Agenda to Change Our Condition

AGENDA TO CHANGE OUR CONDITION

HAMZA YUSUF
& ZAID SHAKIR

SANDALA

AGENDA TO CHANGE OUR CONDITION

SANDALA, INC.
www.sandala.org
info@sandala.org

ISBN 978-0-9855659-1-6

Design: Abdallateef Whiteman

Manufactured in the United States of America

CONTENTS

بسم الله الرحمن الرحيم

Introduction

ISLAM IS SUBMISSION to what is Real. It is a recognition and an acceptance of the way things really are, and not as they appear. Everything is in submission to Allah, who is the Real (al-Ḥaqq). Only human beings and willful spirits (jinn) can rebel against our Creator. Over fourteen hundred years ago, this path of islam[1] was renewed to mark the entry into the last phase of human experience on earth. It was renewed by the best of creation, the Prophet Muḥammad ﷺ as the final Prophet and the seal of all Allah's prophets, upon them all be peace. He was its greatest wayfarer, and he never deviated from its course. His blessed footprints remain clear and unchanged for anyone desiring to set out on that ancient prophetic path.

Before you is a concise treatise on the path to *taqwā* (conscious awareness of our Lord). Devotion to God through *taqwā* is the primary reason for our existence and the means by which we are ensured continued succor from our Creator.

Allah says in the first command in the entire Qur'an:

يَٰٓأَيُّهَا ٱلنَّاسُ ٱعْبُدُوا۟ رَبَّكُمُ ٱلَّذِى خَلَقَكُمْ وَٱلَّذِينَ
مِن قَبْلِكُمْ لَعَلَّكُمْ تَتَّقُونَ

O humanity, worship your Lord,
who created you and those before you,
in order for you to realize taqwā (2:21)

In the first prohibition, we read:

فَلَا تَجْعَلُوا۟ لِلَّهِ أَندَادًا وَأَنتُمْ تَعْلَمُونَ

Do not set up false deities beside Allah,
you are aware of what you are doing (2:22)

While there are many false deities beside Allah, the self is the greatest and most subtle:

أَرَءَيْتَ مَنِ ٱتَّخَذَ إِلَـٰهَهُۥ هَوَىٰهُ

Have you not seen the one
who took his desire as his deity? (25:43)

Struggle with the self is the means by which we purify our hearts of false deities. It is the ancient way of the prophets. It is to walk the path toward a realized state of submission to the will of Allah.

Our God is mighty and transcendent, exalted above and beyond the pettiness of this lower world, but He is also an immanent Lord who sustains and nourishes His creation at every level of existence:

يَـٰٓأَيُّهَا ٱلْإِنسَـٰنُ مَا غَرَّكَ بِرَبِّكَ ٱلْكَرِيمِ ۞ ٱلَّذِى خَلَقَكَ فَسَوَّىٰكَ

فَعَدَلَكَ ۞ فِىٓ أَىِّ صُورَةٍ مَّا شَآءَ رَكَّبَكَ

O humanity, what has caused you to be deluded
about your generous Lord who has created you
and made you so perfectly proportioned
and fashioned you in whatever form He chose? (82:6–8)

OUR CURRENT STATE

Now the current state of the people of this ancient path is deplorable. Generally speaking, we are powerless, bereft, morally bankrupt—objects of history rather than subjects of history, as were our pious predecessors who engaged the world with the power of truth and dispelled darkness with their spiritual light. Our condition is far from that of our noble forbearers. It is as if we never recited or even heard the prayer of our Prophet ﷺ, which he recited every morning:

اللَّهُمَّ إِنِّي أَعُوذُ بِكَ مِنَ الْهَمِّ وَالْحَزَنِ ، وَالْعَجْزِ وَالْكَسَلِ ، وَالْجُبْنِ وَالْبُخْلِ ، وَضَلَعِ الدَّيْنِ ، وَغَلَبَةِ الرِّجَالِ

O Allah, I seek refuge in you from grief and anxiety, impotence and indolence, cowardice and miserliness, and from being overcome by debt and overpowered by men.[2]

The question arises: *How did we reach this state?* Before responding to this question, we should ask a more important one: *How do we get out of this state?* The answers to both questions are painful and complex. However, we can bypass all of the ramifications of both answers and arrive at a simple yet profound summative response:

إِنَّ ٱللَّهَ لَا يُغَيِّرُ مَا بِقَوْمٍ حَتَّىٰ يُغَيِّرُوا۟ مَا بِأَنفُسِهِمْ

Allah does not change a people
until they change what is in themselves. (13:11)

According to Imam Abū Ṭālib al-Makkī in *The Nourishment of the Heart*,[3] the beauty of this verse is that it comprises a twofold meaning. First, it means that Allah does not remove blessings that He has bestowed upon a people until they transgress from obedience to disobedience. This is the response to our first question: We are in this state because of our disobedience. In other words, we exchanged guidance for misguidance, and Allah left us to fend for ourselves. The second meaning of this verse is that Allah does not change a peoples' outward state of abasement, humiliation, and abjection until they change what is in themselves. This answers our second question: To get out of this state, we must consciously move from a state of disobedience to a state of obedience. We must recognize that Allah gave us guidance through Messengers—in our case, the final Prophet ﷺ—and that as long as we adhered to that guidance in large numbers, we were under the protection of Allah. As those numbers diminished throughout Muslim history, the outward enemies of Islam began to make inroads into the heartland of the Muslims until they actually conquered the Muslim lands—but this had been preceded by an onslaught of inward enemies who began to make inroads into our hearts. Today, both the Muslim heartland and Muslim hearts are oppressed by inward and outward forces that oppose the purpose of Islam, which is to free people from submission to created things by helping them achieve submission to the Creator of things. A culture of vice, usury, and consumption that enslaves people to the lowest aspects of their nature cannot survive amid large numbers of people committed to freeing themselves from those aspects of their nature.

The earlier manifestations of such dark forces that succeeded in penetrating the Muslim lands also set up schools to inculcate their ideas and ways into the hearts of the young, impressionable Muslims of the last two centuries. They undermined the spiritual authority of the scholars of Islam, making them appear backward and foolish by promoting the idea that the scholars' religious cosmologies paled before the impressive pillars of modern science and industry. They then began to remove the powerful cultural distinctions of Muslims that had flourished for centuries and replace them with the accoutrements of Western experimental cultural norms and mores.

Slowly, the dress of Muslims changed; the scarves fell from the heads of our women and the beards from the faces of our men. Robes and modest dress were replaced first by ridiculous brimmed hats, starched suits and ties, and finally by jeans and T-shirts, causing Muslims to appear not as caliphs of Allah but as wage-slaves of the Western-styled factories that sprouted up all over the world. Sandals, so beloved to the Prophet of Allah ﷺ, were replaced with tennis shoes made in sweatshops by people so poor that they could not afford the very shoes they produced.

One need only look at the photographs taken by the first Europeans in the lands of Islam one hundred years ago to see the nobility of Muslim dress. The American poet Ezra Pound remarked that he had no idea of the force that was unleashed from the Arabian Peninsula in the seventh century that led to a thousand mosques in Cordoba, Spain, until he caught a glimpse of it in the way a Muslim walked in Tangier in 1913. Compare that image to the current Muslim cities teeming with desolate youth looking for a ticket out of their empty lives to anywhere but home.

Muslim cuisine, once the envy of the world, produced in the homes of the believers with love and remembrance of Allah's blessings, is being replaced with techno-food, which is not produce or livestock but a pre-packaged product bereft of *barakah* (blessing). Muslims have forgotten that food is the foundation of behavior, according to our scholars' understanding of Allah's words:

يَـٰٓأَيُّهَا ٱلرُّسُلُ كُلُوا۟ مِنَ ٱلطَّيِّبَـٰتِ وَٱعْمَلُوا۟ صَـٰلِحًا ۖ

O you Messengers, eat of pure things,
and do righteous deeds. (23:51)

Pure food is being replaced with fast food made with haste and waste, two attributes of the devil. Sugared sodas replace natural milk, water, and juice. Corporate fast food chains, with their mass-produced, disease-ridden, pathogenic food, now appear everywhere, even in the sacred cities of Mecca and Medina. Meanwhile, Muslims, who for centuries ate food filled with *barakah*, made by people with loving hearts who found joy in feeding others, now line up to consume "products" with less nutritional value than dog or cat food.

While the premodern Muslim world had many problems, we see in the heartland remnants of cities that were once centers of learning, culture, commerce, and trade, as well as examples of some of the most stunning architecture, gardens, and parks that engendered awe in the eyes of all who gazed upon them. Those great testimonies of Islam's solidarity and Muslim vitality are now largely ruins that have been replaced by the most hideous and poorly designed cement houses and buildings, ready to collapse at the slightest tremor. Houses once filled with the remembrance of Allah, love of His Prophet ﷺ, and love of the Prophet's family and friends, are now filled with empty films and the sound of television programming antithetical to the values and morals that buttressed the Islamic civilizational enterprise.

Beautiful and inspiring *madrasahs* (schools), where the love of Allah and His Prophet ﷺ was instilled in the hearts of the students along with a rich understanding of the *dīn* (religion) of Allah and with memorizations of His Book, have been replaced by secular institutions that instill in people a disdain for the past and a boredom that lingers long after the last empty book is closed and an equally empty career begun.

This is our state. Division reigns supreme—distrust, suspicion, and conspiracy theories linger in our communities, and we blame everyone but our own selves for our present condition. Most Muslims now live under the yoke of tyrannical governments that, through abusive systems of rule, generate an indolence and lassitude that make Muslims among the least productive people on earth. The religion has become a refuge for angry youth who use it as a political platform to rage against the injustices of the West; they should instead remind people what the visionary Mālik b. Nabī said over half a century ago: The colonial West is nothing but "a scavenger on an already moribund carcass." If Muslims were truly living Islam, our greatness would dispel any negative influence from the West in the traditional lands of Islam.

We must also remember that neither Americans nor Western people are our enemies per se and that if they knew what Islam truly is, many of them would either embrace Islam or at least have a healthy respect for it and its virtues. Some, like the eminent historian Arnold Toynbee, even recognize in it a spiritual power that could help reinvigorate the dissipated state of society and its life-threatening social ills. No doubt, dark elements in every society oppose true Islam, but they are a minority and in no way represent the interests of the broader society. As long as Muslims attack the nebulous "West" as the sole enemy of Islam, we only reveal our own bankruptcy and inability to present the clear and clement message of Islam to people who, for the first time in history, are not only receptive to it but actually invite Muslims to tell them about it and enable Muslims to use the airways and Internet to take it into their cars and homes.

Our beloved Prophet ﷺ asked only one thing of the Quraysh: "Let me be that I may invite people to Islam."[4] They did not acquiesce. We, on the other hand, are given leave to invite people, yet we do not. This is not to deny that there are some who oppose the spread of Islam. Among such people are those who will not sit idly by and allow others to invite people to Islam without attempting to undermine Muslims, cause dissension in the ranks of believers, and place obstacles along the path. They ultimately manifest disbelief in a very real way, and their existence is a test from Allah to distinguish real believers from hypocrites. However, our Prophet ﷺ, in a sound hadith said, "Do not seek confrontation with your enemies, but when it occurs, be steadfast."[5]

True Muslims love peace, obey the law, but are also commanded by Allah to be witnesses unto humanity. In order to fulfill this, we must first be witnesses unto ourselves:

أَتَأْمُرُونَ ٱلنَّاسَ بِٱلْبِرِّ وَتَنسَوْنَ أَنفُسَكُمْ

Do you command people to righteousness
and forget yourselves? (2:44)

INNER AND OUTER TRANSFORMATIONS

The path for us in these Western lands is twofold: The first is inner transformation through spiritual struggle with the soul. The second is outer transformation through struggle with the vices and degrading aspects of society—this means working toward the realization of social justice and a culture that embodies moral comportment, protects children, and enhances family and community life.

The majority of this book pertains to the first path—the path to *taqwā*. The first four chapters elucidate a simple yet effective means to transform our inner world. The final chapter affirms the necessity of civic involvement and productive work in the outer world. Both these paths are in accordance with the aims and the purpose of Allah's creation. According to Rāghib al-Isbahānī, there are two main reasons why Allah created human beings. The first is to worship Allah, which is only completed with inward purity:

وَمَآ أُمِرُوٓا۟ إِلَّا لِيَعْبُدُوا۟ ٱللَّهَ مُخْلِصِينَ لَهُ ٱلدِّينَ حُنَفَآءَ

They were only commanded to worship Allah with purity,
making the religion solely for Him. (98:5)

The second reason is to cultivate the world:

هُوَ أَنشَأَكُم مِّنَ ٱلْأَرْضِ وَٱسْتَعْمَرَكُمْ فِيهَا

He brought you forth from the earth
and has caused you to cultivate it. (11:61)

"Cultivation" here means to sow seeds that produce both temporal fruits as well as eternal ones. Such cultivation entails building schools, hospitals, farms, roads, bridges, and cities and towns wherein Allah is worshiped and the sanctity of the earth is preserved.

In order for us to realize our God-given potential within our lifetimes, we must break the cycles of stagnation by abandoning methods that have proven ineffective in fulfilling our responsibilities as people committed to Islam. We can accomplish this only by changing our current condition—this requires courage, commitment, and above all, critical introspection.

THE IMPORTANCE OF FAMILY

The family is the first and most important unit of society and is designed to nurture and prepare the young to carry on the civilizational enterprise. It is in serious crisis throughout the world, and our children, whether in Muslim households or those of other faiths and beliefs, are suffering everywhere. Schools once meant to nourish and enhance the intellects, bodies, and souls of our youth, now dumb them down and prepare them for a life of mediocrity and servility—in many instances to perform meaningless jobs that neither benefit humanity nor help the individual grow morally and spiritually. Government is now encroaching on every aspect of our lives. Privacy, once honored and respected in all societies, is breached daily by sophisticated technology capable of monitoring virtually everything we do.

We will need to assume a tremendous responsibility to change the state of our families. We must raise our children outside of the modern schools that are designed to make them no more than functional literates. We absolutely must remove our children from state schools and design, build, and support life-enhancing places of learning. It is also imperative to abandon cruel and punitive child rearing techniques, as this is the primary source of social dysfunction and hypocrisy. The eminent scholar, Imam Ibn Khaldūn, identified this problem in the *Muqaddimah*:

> Severe punishment in the course of instruction does harm to the student, especially to little children, because it is among the things that make for bad habits. Students, bondsmen, and servants who are raised with injustice and arbitrary force are overwhelmed by it. It causes them to feel oppressed and results in inertia. It makes them indolent and induces them to lie and be insincere. That is, their outward behavior differs from what they are thinking or feeling. This is because they fear that if they tell the truth, they will be punished and will suffer tyrannical treatment. Thus, they learn deceit and trickery. This becomes habitual and part of their character.
>
> They lose that attribute that accompanies all social and political organizations and gives people their humanity, namely, the ability to protect and defend themselves and their homes, and they in turn become dependent on others for this. Indeed, their souls become lazy and lose the desire to acquire the virtues and qualities of good character. This invariably causes them to fall short of their human potential and never realize their humanity. As a result, they revert to the *lowest of the low* [Qur'an, 95:5]. This is what has happened to every people who have come under the yoke of tyranny and learned through it the meaning of injustice. We can easily prove this by simply observing anyone who is not in control of his own affairs and has no authority on his side to guarantee his personal well being.[6]

Many parents employ internalized tyrannical control models in child rearing. Unfortunately, those who grow up in despotic cultures often internalize those same governing patterns in their homes. In fact, congruence theory illustrates how the aggregate of homes that make up a society is inevitably a reflection of the same patterns of authority used in other social institutions, including and most importantly the government. If the model that the government employs is despotic, this is merely a reflection of despotic families that make up the society and is the meaning of the prophetic statement, "As you are, so are the people placed in charge of you."[7] Unfortunately, when Muslims migrate to Western countries in search of more political and circumstantial freedom in their affairs, some of them end up replicating in their own homes the same models of authority that caused them to flee their countries in the first place.

Our children are our future and our legacy. We must take back the divine and inalienable right to raise and nurture them with love and fairness. Our Prophet ﷺ never subjected his children to punitive treatments that destroy initiative and volition in a child:

لَّقَدْ كَانَ لَكُمْ فِى رَسُولِ ٱللَّهِ أُسْوَةٌ حَسَنَةٌ لِّمَن كَانَ
يَرْجُوا۟ ٱللَّهَ وَٱلْيَوْمَ ٱلْءَاخِرَ وَذَكَرَ ٱللَّهَ كَثِيرًا

You have in the Messenger of Allah a perfect example for one who seeks Allah, and [forgiveness] *on the Last Day, and does much remembrance of Allah.* (33:21)

Nor were the Prophet's children subject to the inadequate education represented in many modern schools. This in no way implies that all schooling is bad, but most of the schools that presently exist are more effective in stunting the intellectual, spiritual, and social growth of our youth than in nurturing them. Home schooling is a viable option that should be seriously considered, and it has proven over the centuries to be one of the most effective means of educating a healthy and benevolent child.

Our hope is that this manual be taken seriously. It is rooted in the Book, the Sunnah (prophetic tradition), and the example of our pious predecessors. We hope that you will commit to implementing it to the best of your ability and that you find a group of brothers or sisters to work together with you. According to the well-known hadith, "Allah will continue to assist the servant, so long as the servant is assisting his brother."[8]

Allah says at the end of the Qur'anic chapter entitled "The Spider,"

وَٱلَّذِينَ جَٰهَدُواْ فِينَا لَنَهۡدِيَنَّهُمۡ سُبُلَنَاۚ وَإِنَّ ٱللَّهَ لَمَعَ ٱلۡمُحۡسِنِينَ

Those who struggle in Our way,
We guide them to Our paths,
and Allah is with the people of excellence. (29:69)

Imam Sāwī, in his magisterial commentary of the Qur'an, says, "This verse was revealed before martial jihad was prescribed, as it is a Meccan verse; therefore, the meaning of jihad in the verse is 'struggle with one's own soul.'"

Imam al-Ḥasan said, "Jihad is to go against one's desire." Fuḍayl b. ʿIyyād said the verse means, "Those who struggle in acquiring knowledge, We will guide them to the paths of acting according to it." Sahl b. ʿAbd Allāh said it means, "Those who struggle in obeying Us, We will guide them to the paths of Our rewards."

It is also said that this verse means, "Those who struggle for Our sake according to what they know, We will guide them to what they do not know." This is based upon the hadith that states, "Whoever acts according to his knowledge, Allah will grant him knowledge he did not know."[9] The greatest jihad is the struggle with one's self for the sake of Allah, and those who do so are promised this guidance and help from Allah for their efforts. Now is the time to set out on the greater jihad with the provision of trust, the armor of the Book and Sunnah, the steed of health, and the sword of resolve.

A man once came to a sage and said, "I think your path is a wonderful path, but it is too arduous for me to follow." The sage responded, "Most people attempt something before they give it up, but you have already defined your limits before testing them."[10]

The path of Allah is indeed arduous, and it would appear to one looking at it that treading it is too difficult for most of us. Let us set out first and then see how long we can last. God willing, a divine wind will blow on our backs, our feet will become light, and wondrous fellow wayfarers will show up with sustenance just when we thought we had none. Our success is by Allah, upon Him we place our trust, and to Him do we return.

Hamza Yusuf
Sandala, Inc., 2007

ENDNOTES

1. When spelled with a lowercase "i," islam refers to the willful submission to Allah as a general concept. When spelled with an uppercase "I," Islam refers to the willful submission to Allah codified as the religion that was revealed to the Prophet Muḥammad ﷺ.
2. Imam Abū ʿAbd Allāh b. Muḥammad al-Bukhārī, *Ṣaḥīḥ al-Bukhārī* (Sidon: al-Maktabah al-ʿAṣriyyah, 1426/2005), p.1139, no.6369.
3. Abū Ṭālib al-Makkī, *Qūt al-qulūb* (Beirut: Dār al-Badr, 1995).
4. Imam Abū ʿAbd Allāh Aḥmad b. Ḥanbal, *Musnad al-Imam Aḥmad* (Cairo: Dār al-Maymaniyyah, 1313/1895), 5:427.
5. Imam Muslim b. al-Ḥajjāj, *Ṣaḥīḥ Muslim* (Dār Iḥyā' al-Turāth al-ʿArabī, 1420/2000), p.781, no.1742.
6. Ibn Khaldūn, *al-Muqaddimah* (Cairo: Dār al-Shaʿb, 1381/1961), p.508.
7. Imam Ismāʿīl b. Muḥammad al-ʿAjlūnī, *Kashf al-khafā'* (Beirut: Dār Iḥyā' al-Turāth al-ʿArabī, 1352/1933), 2:126–127, no.1997.
8. Imam Muḥyī al-Dīn b. Sharaf al-Nawawī, *al-Minhāj: Sharḥ Ṣaḥīḥ Muslim* (Beirut: Dār al-Maʿrifah, 1998), 9:24, no.2793.
9. Imam Abū Nuʿaym Aḥmad b. ʿAbd Allāh al-Iṣfahānī, *Ḥilyat al-awliyā'* (Beirut: Dār al-Fikr, 1996), 10:15. Abū Nuʿaym mentions that this saying should be more accurately attributed to the Prophet Ibn Maryam (Jesus) ﷺ. Allah knows best.
10. Ibid. Abū Nuʿaym mentions that this narration also is more properly attributed to the Prophet Jesus ﷺ. The chain of narration that attributes it to the Prophet Muḥammad ﷺ from Imam Aḥmad is not reliable.

1

Taqwā: Its Definition and Benefits

SĪDĪ ʿABD AL-WĀḤID B. ʿĀSHIR defines *taqwā* as follows: "The summation of *taqwā* is avoiding prohibitions and fulfilling injunctions both inwardly and outwardly."

In his book of definitions, Imam al-Jurjānī defines it accordingly:

> Linguistically, it means, "to ward off." In other words, it is "to take precaution." According to the scholars of truth, it is "to protect oneself from the punishment of Allah by obedience to Him." It is "to guard the self from Allah's punishment due to an omission of a right action or commission of a wrong action." What is intended in one's obedience is sincerity.[1]

Ibn ʿĀshir says, "Its aspects are four in number, and these for the wayfarer are the pathways of benefit." Accordingly, the four pathways of benefit are as follows:

- fulfilling obligations outwardly;
- fulfilling obligations inwardly;
- avoiding prohibitions outwardly; and
- avoiding prohibitions inwardly.

Thus, the wayfarer on the path to purification and success is someone committed to struggling with these four matters, which must be applied to eight things—the heart and the following inroads to the heart possessed by the vast majority of humanity: the tongue, eyes, ears, stomach, genitals, hands, and feet.

A human being is responsible for all of these, and if one is vigilant about them and struggles to guard them, then he or she is on a path to achieving *taqwā*.

There are five stations according to Imam Ibn Juzayy al-Kalbī:

- guarding against disbelief—this is the station of submission;
- guarding against forbidden things—this is the station of repentance;
- guarding against doubtful matters—this is the station of scrupulousness;
- guarding against extraneous matters—this is the station of freedom (*zuhd*); and
- guarding against other than Allah occupying the heart—this is the station of vigilance.[2]

Every believer is at the station of submission, but we increase Allah's protection over us by attaining the higher stations. Because the vast majority of the Muslim community is only at the first or the second level, we all suffer. When a critical mass of believers commits to moving to the third and the fourth levels, we will see the benefits of *taqwā* permeate our communities, as promised in the Qur'an.

BENEFITS OF *TAQWĀ*

The benefits of *taqwā* are innumerable, and many are hidden to humanity. Only Allah knows all of the benefits, but many are mentioned in the Qur'an; the most salient ones are below.

The moral rectitude of one's offspring:

يَٰبُنَيَّ أَقِمِ ٱلصَّلَوٰةَ وَأۡمُرۡ بِٱلۡمَعۡرُوفِ وَٱنۡهَ عَنِ ٱلۡمُنكَرِ وَٱصۡبِرۡ عَلَىٰ مَآ أَصَابَكَۖ إِنَّ ذَٰلِكَ
مِنۡ عَزۡمِ ٱلۡأُمُورِ

O my son! Establish regular prayer, enjoin what is just, and forbid what is wrong. And bear with patient constancy whatever afflicts you; surely this is resolve in your affairs. (31:17)

Another verse, according to one interpretation, states:

وَلۡيَخۡشَ ٱلَّذِينَ لَوۡ تَرَكُواْ مِنۡ خَلۡفِهِمۡ ذُرِّيَّةً ضِعَٰفًا
خَافُواْ عَلَيۡهِمۡ فَلۡيَتَّقُواْ ٱللَّهَ

Those who have left behind weak offspring are fearful concerning their well-being; let them have consciousness of Allah. (4:9)

Blessings come from above and below:

وَلَوْ أَنَّ أَهْلَ ٱلْقُرَىٰٓ ءَامَنُوا۟ وَٱتَّقَوْا۟ لَفَتَحْنَا عَلَيْهِم بَرَكَـٰتٍ
مِّنَ ٱلسَّمَآءِ وَٱلْأَرْضِ

Had only the people of the cities believed and had taqwā,
We would have opened up for them blessings from
the heavens and the earth. (7:96)[3]

Provision from Allah and a way out of difficult circumstances:

وَمَن يَتَّقِ ٱللَّهَ يَجْعَل لَّهُۥ مَخْرَجًا ۞ وَيَرْزُقْهُ مِنْ حَيْثُ لَا يَحْتَسِبُ

Whoever has taqwā,
We will prepare for him a way out and provide for him
from where he was not expecting. (65:2)

Safety:

وَأَنجَيْنَا ٱلَّذِينَ ءَامَنُوا۟ وَكَانُوا۟ يَتَّقُونَ

We saved those who believed in Us
and had been people of taqwā. (27:53)

The divine presence, manifested as Allah's protection:

إِنَّ ٱللَّهَ مَعَ ٱلَّذِينَ ٱتَّقَوا۟ وَّٱلَّذِينَ هُم مُّحْسِنُونَ

Surely Allah is with those who have taqwā
and who beautify with excellence. (16:128)

Victory:

وَمَن يُطِعِ ٱللَّهَ وَرَسُولَهُۥ وَيَخْشَ ٱللَّهَ وَيَتَّقْهِ فَأُو۟لَـٰٓئِكَ هُمُ ٱلْفَآئِزُونَ

Whoever obeys Allah and His Messenger
and knowingly has awe and consciousness of Allah,
those are the victors. (24:52)

A goodly end to life:

وَإِنَّ لِلْمُتَّقِينَ لَحُسْنَ مَـَٔابٍ

Surely for the people of taqwā
is a beautiful end. (38:49)

Paradise itself:

تِلْكَ ٱلْجَنَّةُ ٱلَّتِى نُورِثُ مِنْ عِبَادِنَا مَن كَانَ تَقِيًّا

That is the Garden, and We give it
to whoever of Our servants had taqwā. (19:63)

These benefits should suffice for any believer to desire to become a person of *taqwā*.

ACHIEVING *TAQWĀ*

The only way to achieve the station of *taqwā* is through spiritual struggle (*mujāhadah*).

Spiritual struggle is not something that miraculously comes into one's life. It is a move of the heart that begins to affect the limbs and then results in sincere repentance (*tawbah*), in which we seek to purify ourselves of prior wrongs and remove them from our present activities and make a strong commitment to a future free of the mistakes of the past.

Allah has commanded us as a unified community to turn to Him with sincerity, and this is what we must do:

وَتُوبُوٓا۟ إِلَى ٱللَّهِ جَمِيعًا أَيُّهَ ٱلْمُؤْمِنُونَ لَعَلَّكُمْ تُفْلِحُونَ

O you who believe! Turn to Allah, all of you together,
with sincerity in order for you to have success. (24:31)

With sincere commitment, we can accomplish this greatest of human tasks, which is, in the final analysis, our sole purpose for being alive.

Allah's first command in His Book is:

يَـٰٓأَيُّهَا ٱلنَّاسُ ٱعْبُدُوا۟ رَبَّكُمُ ٱلَّذِى خَلَقَكُمْ وَٱلَّذِينَ
مِن قَبْلِكُمْ لَعَلَّكُمْ تَتَّقُونَ

O humanity, worship your Lord,
who created you and those before you,
in order for you to realize taqwā (2:21)

This is our purpose for being here. We must simply start—not tomorrow or the day after—but today, right now, at this moment.

The heart must make a firm commitment and never turn back. The rewards are immense; the pleasure of mastering the self is second only to the subtle knowledge and pleasure of intimacy with Allah that is a result of that mastery.

What follows is a series of exercises designed to help us set out on the path. They are difficult, but earning paradise was never meant to be easy. All things of worth are only obtained through great effort, whether the pearl at the bottom of the ocean or the skill of the master craftsman. The pleasure of our Lord is infinitely greater than the material gains of this world.

First, we begin the forthcoming section, a study on the heart that is taken largely from the scholar and stalwart Qadi Abū Bakr.[4] We need to internalize its meanings and ask Allah to give us success in purifying our hearts. The heart will be transformed through remembrance of Allah, halal work, and guarding our five daily prayers along with the eight physical inroads.

Next, we need to make a commitment to read and practice the exercises. Finally, we set out today with the intention to achieve our goal: *taqwā.*

May Allah give us the success to be people of *taqwā.* May He unite the hearts of this community in love of Him and His beloved Messenger ﷺ. May He guide us to the path of *taqwā* and give us both the courage and the success to be among its people. May He raise among us people who enjoin goodness and forbid evil out of love for human well-being and not hate—out of desire for people to draw near to their Lord and not from anger in their hearts. May He remove rancor, enmity, and resentment from the hearts of the believers.

ٱلْحَمْدُ لِلَّهِ رَبِّ ٱلْعَـٰلَمِينَ

Praise be to the Lord of all the worlds. (1:2)

ENDNOTES

1. Imam al-Jurjānī, *al-Taʿrīfāt* (Beirut: Dār al-Kitāb al-ʿArabī, n.d.), p.90.
2. Ibn Juzayy, *al-Tashīl* (Beirut: Dār al-Arqām, n.d.), 1:69.
3. How different is this state of blessings coming from above and below from the bombs that now fall on our heads from above and the droughts and civil strife on our earth due to our lack of *taqwā*!
4. This is the famous Mālikī jurist, Qur'an commentator, and hadith expert who is considered a *mujtahid murajjiḥ* in the Mālikī school and is recognized by all scholars of Islam as an authority on the sciences of Islam. He died in 543 AH in the city of Fez, Morocco. He is not to be confused with the Andalusian scholar, Muḥyī al-Dīn b. al-ʿArabī.

2

The Heart and Its Treatment

FACILITATING ACTION BASED UPON TRUE KNOWLEDGE

ACTION HAS TWO modes: the action of the heart and the action of the limbs. As for the heart, there are two concerns: belief (*ʿaqīdah*) and sincerity (*ikhlāṣ*).

Belief

Sound belief is accomplished by removing any doubtful matters from the heart. This is easy, by the grace of Allah and His gift, and throughout the ages many people have accomplished it.

Sincerity

It is extremely difficult to achieve sincerity of the heart through the actions of the limbs. The entire creation was at a standstill when it heard the words of the Creator:

وَمَآ أُمِرُوٓاْ إِلَّا لِيَعۡبُدُواْ ٱللَّهَ مُخۡلِصِينَ لَهُ ٱلدِّينَ حُنَفَآءَ

They were only commanded to worship Allah sincerely (mukhliṣīn), with the religion solely for Him. (98:5)

Allah also says,

أَلَا لِلَّهِ ٱلدِّينُ ٱلۡخَالِصُ

Is not the sincere religion (al-dīn al-khāliṣ) solely for Allah? (39:3)

The Arabic word *khulūṣ* means "purity," and the term *laban khāliṣ* means "milk that is free of impurities." This is the milk taken from the animal before it is contaminated with anything else.

The heart's purity is contaminated by wrong actions and can only be purified by repentance and remorse. Purity comprises a great station in the religion, just as fornication, for example, is a precipitous fall into wrong action.

Scholars of the heart have identified both corrupting and purifying actions that affect the heart's state. This text focuses on what facilitates the path to purity and how to draw near the way of struggle with the commanding soul. Moreover, it clarifies matters that edify the way to free one's intention from any contingencies that cause one to act for the sake of anyone or anything other than Allah.

The likeness of the one who acts for the sake of anyone or anything other than Allah is described in the following example. A shop owner hires a laborer and says to him, "This is my shop, and this is my work. Therefore, do all your work in my best interests." Despite this decree, the laborer performs his work in the best interests of someone else or himself, rather than those of the owner. As Muslims, we cannot do Allah's work and bidding when we have only our own worldly interests at the forefront.

How then can we remove worldly motivations from our actions? The answer lies in the rectification of our intentions. Actions are only in accordance with intentions, and thus starting with the intention behind an act is the beginning of achieving a state of living for the sake of Allah. If one applies perfume, it can be done in order to follow the Sunnah of the Prophet ﷺ and also as an act of charity for others. When it is intended to be "for the angels of my Lord and in adherence to the tradition of my Prophet ﷺ," we take a permitted act and elevate it to a recommended or obligatory one. Likewise, food should not be eaten merely for pleasure. We should intend the energy derived from the food to be used for the strengthening of our bodies to better serve Allah.

The following hadith emphasizes the importance of intending our actions for the sake of Allah:

> The first people to be judged on the Day of Resurrection are the following: a man who was martyred, who is brought into the divine presence and shown his blessings, who admits to them, and who is asked "What did you do with all these blessings?" He will reply, "I fought for Your sake and was martyred." Allah, the Exalted, will say, "You lie! You fought to be called a courageous man, and

it was said about you [and thus you have been recompensed]." It is then ordered that he be taken to the Fire.

Then someone who studied the Qur'an and taught it is brought into the divine presence and shown his blessings, and he acknowledges them and then is asked what he did with them. He responds, "I studied knowledge and transmitted it, and I recited the Qur'an for Your sake." It is said to him, "You lie! Rather you desired to be called learned, and it was said about you." It is then ordered that he be taken to the Fire, and be dragged along his face and thrust into it.[1]

The hadith continues, and at the end of the narration a generous man who gave to be known as generous is met with the same fate.

ACHIEVING SINCERITY

One of the most effective ways to achieve sincerity and remove blemishes from our intentions is to guard our tongues and always speak truthfully. When we fail to recognize the impoverishment of our inward reality and the disparity between what we think and feel and what we communicate to others, we become odious to Allah and His angels. Maintaining one's discourse consistently, in private and public gatherings, is a powerful move toward being sincere. Therefore, the first step toward sincerity of the heart is to protect our tongues from falsehood, dissembling, and prevarications.

Four Sources of the Destructive Qualities of the Tongue

Our tongue expresses our inward state—both our knowledge and our practice. It has only one noble quality, and that is truthfulness. It has over twenty destructive qualities, but they are all rooted in four actions. If you are able to constrain the tongue from engaging in all four, the others are removed with ease.

LYING

Lying or relaying fiction is prohibited in all but three situations:

- as a means to rectify between people;
- as an effective military tactic; or
- when an individual plays with his young children.

However, even the permissibility in the first two cases is through subterfuge and prevarication. It should never be through manifest lies, except in a case where the other party will clearly see through the stratagem. In such circumstances, one may lie with the tongue but must reject it within the heart. Again, this is only applicable in a scenario wherein one's well being or provisions or those of others is endangered. Nevertheless, be cautious with words because a lie might, in some instances, result in a binding obligation.

An example of a case where lying is permitted is that of an oppressor pursuing a just man; in that case, one should deceive the oppressor openly and lead him astray in his search. This is permissible because a lie is not prohibited for its own sake but rather for the harm that is implicit in lying. In such cases, when truthfulness causes greater harm, lying, in its stead, is preferred.

For this reason, the notion that "Good is good for its own sake, and evil is evil for its own sake" is considered false. For example, a murder committed by an aggressor may appear identical to an execution that occurred in compliance with sacred law in both its outward form and its characteristics. Someone who is unaware of what actually transpired might confuse one for the other. Therefore, killing may be just or unjust—it is neither good nor evil per se.

BACKBITING

Backbiting (*ghībah*) is prohibited by the Qur'an, Sunnah, and scholarly consensus. It is defined as mentioning someone in a manner that would upset that person should he hear it, even if it is a true statement about the person. If the statement is untrue, the act is known as calumny. Calumny contains both a lie and backbiting and thus is a greater wrong. Such vices can, in fact, nullify good actions. Allah says:

وَلَا يَغْتَب بَّعْضُكُم بَعْضًا ۚ أَيُحِبُّ أَحَدُكُمْ أَن يَأْكُلَ لَحْمَ أَخِيهِ مَيْتًا فَكَرِهْتُمُوهُ ۚ
وَاتَّقُوا اللَّهَ ۚ إِنَّ اللَّهَ تَوَّابٌ رَّحِيمٌ

Neither allow yourselves to speak ill of one another behind your backs. And would any of you like to eat the flesh of his dead brother? You would hate it! So be conscious of Allah, for Allah is most relenting, most merciful. (49:12)

Likewise, you should detest backbiting because it tears into a person's good name and honor, and this can be much worse than actually tearing off a piece of that person's physical flesh.

In the above verse, Allah likens the absent one to a dead person. The dead person is gone and thus unable to defend himself, just as the absent one being talked about is unable to defend himself. Furthermore, biting off part of something causes harm to it, just as speaking ill of people causes harm to them. A poet said, "A cut inflicted by the tongue is not unlike the cut inflicted by the hand."

Backbiting is permitted only in the following circumstances:

- when appealing to an authority to remove an injustice;
- when seeking help from others to change a wrong or to stop an oppressor from his wrongs;
- when seeking a legal opinion;
- when warning others concerning commerce, marriage, neighbors, and companionship (for example, it is acceptable to mention the violent temperament of a man to his prospective wife);
- when one mentions a man by a nickname he is known by, such as, the "Lamented One" (however, if the nickname is used to belittle him, it is prohibited; if not, then using another name is preferable);
- when mentioning innovation in terms of religious practice (if someone is known for practicing such innovations, then it can be mentioned in relationship to him to warn others, unless there is a valid difference of opinion about the matter, in which case it is strictly prohibited!); or
- when mentioning the wrongs of someone who openly commits those enormities (however, it is prohibited to mention wrongs that others do not know about).

ARGUMENTATION FOR ITS OWN SAKE

Argumentation (*mirā'*) is to dispute using sophistical reasoning, knowing it is fallacious, or to defend a religious innovation intentionally. The innovator argues using verses and sophistry to support an argument in order to present what is false as true.

The Prophet ﷺ said, "Disputation with the Qur'an is disbelief."[2] It is disbelief for the reason that it is one thing for a man to believe his innovation for himself, but to spread it and claim that Allah shares his error is not acceptable. Such practice is clearly beyond the pale.

MIRTHFUL JESTING ON SERIOUS OCCASIONS

Jesting and making light of a serious matter is a form of engaging in what is of no concern to anyone. Indeed, abandoning it is deemed an excellent quality. The Prophet ﷺ said, "A beautiful quality in someone's practice of Islam is minding his own business."[3]

Qadi Abū Bakr said,

> I once heard Imam al-Ṭarṭūshī say, "The joker is an ignorant fool because Allah revealed to us a dialogue between the Children of Israel and Moses, upon him be peace: *"Do you take us as the brunt of a joke?"* [asked the Children of Israel. Moses ﷺ] *replied, "I seek refuge in Allah that I should be of the ignorant ones."* [Qur'an, 2:67]

Qadi Abū Bakr also said,

> It would seem to me that if the answer concerns a matter related to religion, then it is ignorance, but if it was some other concern, then it is merely speech. Its ruling is its ruling, and its characteristic is defined by what it contains.

After we have purified our hearts from other than Allah, and our tongues from the aforementioned faults, then we have established firm foundations for divine protection.

The next step on the journey toward sincerity is developing concern for the rest of our responsibilities. Among those, we should focus on ensuring the following two essentials:

- the five foundations of the religion (five pillars of Islam) and
- avoiding mortal sins (*kabā'ir*) vigilantly.

Allah states clearly,

إِن تَجْتَنِبُوا۟ كَبَآئِرَ مَا تُنْهَوْنَ عَنْهُ نُكَفِّرْ عَنكُمْ سَيِّـَٔاتِكُمْ

If you avoid what has been prohibited for you from the enormities, then We will cover over any other wrongs. (4:31)

None truly knows the mortal sins with any certainty except Allah. Indeed, He has concealed them among the prohibited matters. However, some of the masters of knowledge have gathered them and codified them for us. They tally seventeen in number. Abandoning the major sins makes it easier for one to leave lesser wrongs. Likewise, the lesser wrongs that one commits will be removed from one's record through ritual prayers, washings, the hajj, and the lesser pilgrimage (*ʿumrah*).

The Prophet ﷺ said, "One daily prayer to the next and one Friday prayer to the next remit wrong actions as long as enormities are avoided."[4] The hadith clearly states that prayer removes wrongs as long as one avoids mortal sins.

The question arises: Do prayers remove lesser wrongs if we are still engaged in any mortal sins, or does one's engagement in such sins preclude the possibility of the removal of lesser wrongs? The hadith would indicate the first condition, but certainty requires a more cogent proof. Another source seems to strengthen the position that sins are removed:

> If a believing servant performs his ritual cleansing (*wuḍūʾ*), then when he washes his face, the wrongs that resulted from his eyes (looking at the prohibited) are removed with the water, and when he washes his hands, those wrongs are removed with the water or with its last drop. When he washes his feet, then the wrongs acquired from walking where he should not have are removed, until he is free of wrongs.[5]

ENUMERATION OF THE ENORMITIES

FOUR ENORMITIES RELATE TO THE HEART:

- association with Allah (*shirk*);
- perseverance in wrongs, even in lesser ones;
- despair of the mercy of Allah; and
- a false sense of security from the design of Allah.

FOUR ENORMITIES RELATE TO THE TONGUE:

- false testimony (*shahādat al-zūr*);
- accusing others of adultery (*qadhf*);
- sinful oaths (*yamīn ghamūs*); and
- magic (*siḥr*).

THREE ENORMITIES RELATE TO THE STOMACH:

- intake of alcohol or intoxicants;
- consuming the wealth of an orphan; and
- taking interest on wealth.

TWO ENORMITIES RELATE TO THE GENITALS:

- illicit heterosexual relations; and
- homosexual acts.

TWO ENORMITIES RELATE TO THE HANDS:

- killing; and
- theft.

ONE ENORMITY RELATES TO THE FEET:

- fleeing from a battle.

ONE ENORMITY RELATES TO THE WHOLE BODY:

- disrespect of parents.

To consider it from another aspect, one should avoid all the wrongs that relate to or affect any of Allah's servants because those wrongs can be impossible to rectify. As for what remains between an individual and Allah, this is less harmful to others and is much easier to rectify.

RECOMMENDATIONS FOR REACHING SINCERITY

An excellent practice for achieving sincerity is recitation of the Qur'an with reflection. If unable to contemplate its relevance to oneself or one's actions, then simply recite it. The difference between the two is illustrated in the following anecdote:

> A king sends a letter to his governors. In it, he commands them to fortify their capitols, guard the boundaries of the kingdom, act justly toward their citizens, judge with equity between them, give every man his due, and attend well to all other governmental concerns.
>
> When the letter arrives to the various governors, there are two responses. Some receive it with great respect and reverence, read it with excellent understanding, and set about implementing its injunctions and fulfilling its commands. The others receive it with respect and reverence and place it at the foremost of their concerns. They fail, however, to understand it and thus do not implement its injunctions, nor fulfill its commands.

Let us imagine the two groups when they are called before the king. What will their respective states be?

In addition to reciting the Qur'an, we must concern ourselves with the appropriate supplications and litanies in their respective times and places, and use only sound transmissions concerning those matters. We must not engage in litanies that do not have a strong foundation. Indeed, if Satan is unable to occupy us with other than the remembrance of Allah, then he will attempt to seduce us into using formulas that are innovative and have no foundation.

If Allah wills, we will be able to follow all these matters, He will open the doors of His mercy to us, wisdom will flow from our tongues, the ability to obey Him in what remains of our responsibilities will be made easy for us, and we will be called great in the dominion of the heavens.

May Allah count us among those who seek knowledge and wisdom, who concern themselves with the Book of Allah and respect what it contains, and who transmit it to others and cause them to understand it. As the Prophet ﷺ said, "The best of you are those who learn the Qur'an and teach it."[6]

ENDNOTES

1. *Ṣaḥīḥ Muslim*, pp.854–855, no.1905.
2. *Musnad al-Imam Aḥmad* (Beirut: Mu'assasat al-Risālah, 1420/1999), 13:369, no.7989.
3. *Jāmiʿ al-Tirmidhī*, p.531, no.2317.
4. al-Nawawī, *al-Minhāj*, 2:111, no. 550.
5. Ibid., 2:127, no.576.
6. *Ṣaḥīḥ al-Bukhārī*, p.926, no.5027.

3

Practical Steps to Change Our Condition

THE FIVE PILLARS

FORM A SERIOUS study group to learn the five pillars properly and thoroughly. Once a Muslim reaches adulthood, he or she is in a state of sin until the individual obligations of religion are learned. The five pillars are the starting place. A sound creed must be acquired, followed by the basic knowledge of prayer, zakat, fasting, and pilgrimage. As you learn, practice what you learn. When this is mastered, move on to the rules of marriage, buying and selling, and other relevant sections of sacred law, as your needs dictate.

Commit to a systematic study of the Arabic language, especially the science of *tajwīd* (Qur'anic recitation).[1] Also, study at least one traditional text on the science of purifying the heart, and practice the exercises given to remove the blemishes of the soul. It is preferred that one study with a capable teacher licensed to teach by recognized scholars. In the absence of such a teacher, form a study circle based on humility and the ability to say, "I do not know" when necessary.

ACTIVE OUTREACH

Create an active outreach (*daʿwah*) program designed to produce results. Reach out to the non-Muslim community through teaching, doing community work, and feeding others. At this stage, Muslims need to allay the fears of the dominant community wherever we are minorities. We are not a threat to anyone's safety or well-being. In fact, if we practice our teaching, we are a great blessing to the societies we live in.

We should present Islam at the institutional level, with the aim of educating and informing, not proselytizing. The call to Islam is an invitation, and our communities need to prepare the banquet before inviting the guests. In our personal lives, we should discuss and share our religion with others.

If there are existing organizations already engaged in outreach, do not reinvent the wheel. For instance, for students, there are already many Muslim student groups with outreach programs to support. If there are none, then be the catalyst who starts something.

FOCUS

Find an area of concern that instills a passionate response, and begin to work to alleviate the respective obstacles to produce change in that area. Recognize the power of one. It is Allah's number, and everything good in this world of human endeavors was initially one individual's intention, action, and vision. When there is commitment with sincerity, creation moves to serve the purpose—and we must keep in mind that actions are judged by intentions.

We must also work on changing ourselves while changing the world. If we do not embody the change we wish to see in the world, we have little moral authority in demanding of others what we ourselves fail to practice. We should focus on those areas of neglect in our own selves and commit to constant personal improvement while working on changing our external environment. Internal and external struggles are not mutually exclusive; rather, they complement each other. The deeper and more refined our spiritual state, the greater will be our capacity to deal with the tribulations involved in any worldly endeavor.

We should remember that the greatest struggle is speaking the truth in the presence of unjust authority; this includes the unjust authority of our own lower self when it disobeys Allah. We must constantly remind and rebuke ourselves until we submit.

The internal struggle ("greater" jihad) is struggling to change and purify our own souls, while the external struggle ("lesser" jihad) is striving and struggling to bring about justice and righteousness in our world.[2] We should each identify an area of concern and commit ourselves to improving it. It may be education, the environment, medicine, youth, economics, agriculture, poverty, defense of the oppressed, social equity, or another interest. We should recognize that no one person can perform actively in all of them simultaneously, nor can one be effective by addressing all of them in one lifetime. Therefore, the more we focus, the more effective we can be.

COOPERATION

This religion is based on recognizing the abilities of the believers that constitute the *ummah* (Muslim community) and facilitating the use of their respective gifts. We need to understand that if one person focuses upon an area that differs from our own area of concern, he or she is complementing our own work and not detracting from it by not joining us.

There are many paths to Allah, and He guides those who struggle with themselves for His sake alone. We should not see other Muslims, either individuals or organized groups, as competitors or antagonists. Rather, we should see them as brothers and sisters and either work with them or work separately with amicable relations, the least of which is giving them the greeting of peace with a smile. Our communities suffer from an unhealthy competition, viewing another's failure as our own success. We should all hope and pray for the success of any activity that is good in nature and beneficial to the aims and purposes of sacred law.

Islamic work through diverse organizations should never be the basis for negating the bonds of brotherhood and sisterhood established between us by Islam. When that happens, we are no longer doing Islamic work but are engaged in politics.

We should speak well of other organizations or be silent about them. Once we recognize that most of them are engaged in a different aspect of the same struggle, we come to respect their efforts. If some appear to be or actually are misguided, then we should offer counsel and pray for them. If they have deviant positions or beliefs, then we should request that qualified scholars clarify with clear proofs what those deviations are. In doing so, such a scholar must not use personal opinions but rather those of the rightly-guided scholars of our tradition who are recognized by the scholars of the past.

Rare opinions of one or two scholars that stand in disagreement with the majority of scholars on a given issue must not be used at the cost of unity through diversity, though the opinions may be valid. If it turns out that there is a difference of opinion among our scholars regarding the issue, then we should leave it for the sake of unity and not argue or fight over it. However, if it is indeed wrong by consensus, then we can bring it to their attention wisely and with a sincere desire to help them.

We ought to keep in mind that Moses ﷷ was commanded to go to Pharaoh and *speak to him a gentle word* (20:44).

Remembering that we are not more righteous than Moses ﷷ and that our brother is certainly not farther astray than Pharaoh, we can approach the matter with gentle humility and a genuine desire for the well-being and guidance of all.

We have an example of this gentle approach: when Imam ʿAlī sent Ibn ʿAbbās ﵁ to reason with the Seceders (Khawārij), Ibn ʿAbbās ﵁ succeeded in guiding thousands of them by providing clear proofs. This mass repentance lessened the severity and length of the conflagration when the two forces met on the battlefield.

We cannot view other Muslims as objects of hatred, no matter who they may be. If they are Muslims, they have the sanctity of Islam, and their name is to be honored unless a situation obliges us to condemn an act or position that is in contradistinction to the sacred law and tenets of universal Islam as opposed to sectarian views of Islam.

Moreover, we should not listen to or partake in backbiting Muslims or people of other faiths. If it is necessary to point out deviations to clarify them, we should do so as the Messenger of Allah ﷺ did; on occasion he declared, "What is wrong with a people who do such and such?"

We should also be vigilant in avoiding stale and sterile debates that have persisted for centuries and produce little benefit and much harm.

In addition, we should avoid labeling people or groups as Salafi, Sufi, or Wahhabi, for example, as these engender animosity. Name-calling is condemned in the Qur'an,[3] if the intention is contempt. If the intention is to elucidate a position, then we must examine our intention and also our level of understanding. Most of us are not capable of debating with any legitimate authority whatsoever. Imam al-Rāghib al-Aṣbahānī said, "Disputation is detestable for scholars and those close to Allah, so what is to be said of the argumentation of the uneducated and foolish?"

Consider the words of Allah to His Prophet ﷺ:

وَجَٰدِلْهُم بِٱلَّتِي هِيَ أَحْسَنُ

Debate with them with what is most excellent. (16:125)

Thus, Allah did not permit the Prophet ﷺ to dispute without stipulating that it be with kindness and in a beautiful manner.

Moreover, Allah describes the Prophet ﷺ as being of vast ethical character, and disparages argumentation in His words:

مَا ضَرَبُوهُ لَكَ إِلَّا جَدَلاً

They did not say it except to argue. (43:58)

And in another verse, Allah says:

وَمِنَ ٱلنَّاسِ مَن يُجَٰدِلُ فِي ٱللَّهِ بِغَيْرِ عِلْمٍ وَلَا هُدًى وَلَا كِتَٰبٍ مُّنِيرٍ

From among humanity are those who argue about Allah without knowledge, or guidance, or an illuminating Book. (22:8)

Always heed the advice of Allah:

وَإِذَا رَأَيْتَ ٱلَّذِينَ يَخُوضُونَ فِيٓ ءَايَٰتِنَا فَأَعْرِضْ عَنْهُمْ

If you find those who ignorantly discuss Our signs, then turn away from them. (6:68)

As Imam Mālik said, "Disputation is not from our religion."

GOOD CHARACTER

We must inculcate good character in our daily lives, and always display courteous behavior with Muslims and non-Muslims alike. The most effective outreach is good character. Our Prophet ﷺ said, "I was sent to perfect good character."[4] With good character, people achieve levels of proximity to Allah that even those who are persistent in praying and fasting have a hard time reaching.

KINSHIP

We should strive to maintain excellent kinship bonds and forgive the shortcomings of our relatives for the sake of Allah, in hope that He may forgive our shortcomings. The sacred bonds of blood must never be severed. One of the greatest of the major sins is filial impiety, which is prevalent in modern society. Relationships are a trial from Allah, and the Qur'an reminds us,

وَجَعَلْنَا بَعْضَكُمْ لِبَعْضٍ فِتْنَةً أَتَصْبِرُونَ

We have made some a tribulation for others;
will you show patience? (25:20)

Family is difficult, but the rewards of kindness toward family are immeasurable in this world and only realized in the next. Moreover, the least harm that is accrued from severing kinship bonds is a life of penury.

FAMILIES

We are obliged by sacred law to treat our families, and especially our spouses, with the utmost respect and dignity. The Prophet ﷺ said, "The best of you are those who are the best to their families."[5] A man is judged in this religion by the honor and love he shows his wife and children. Wives should treat their husbands with respect and flexibility. For most women, the spiritual struggle of this life is within the confines of home and family. According to the tradition, to bear this with patience and righteousness is to obtain the reward of a warrior for the sake of Allah. No room whatsoever exists in the Islamic tradition for domestic abuse or violence. A home is a sanctuary and if the wife and children do not feel safe, it is not a Muslim home but a *jāhilī* house. Violence toward family is clearly proscribed in the sacred law, and the blight of domestic violence must be uprooted from our communities.

CHARITY

We should all commit to donating some portion of our wealth in addition to the zakat that we pay. Commit to some Islamic cause financially, and support it on a regular basis. Also, try to support any bona fide organization that solicits help. Regular spending in charity diminishes the value of the world in our hearts. This is one of the greatest means to prepare us to meet our Lord. The Prophet ﷺ said, "Wealth is not diminished by charity."[6]

QUR'AN

Read the Qur'an in its entirety at least twice a year—at least once in Ramadan and once during the rest of the year. Try to read it with contemplation at least once a year. We should make it a habit to read those chapters the Prophet ﷺ encouraged us to read every day at their appropriate times. "Yā Sīn," "al-Mulk," and "al-Wāqiʿah" should be a part of a daily spiritual practice. If one is able, one should complete the Qur'an every forty days, every month, or every week, as was the profound practice of our earlier communities.

We should also commit to memorizing some portion of the Qur'an every year and couple that with memorizing *The Forty Hadith* of Imam al-Nawawī. Also, reading *The Gardens of the Righteous* at least once a year is a cogent way of reminding ourselves of daily Sunnah practices. We should all strive to retain what we have memorized from the Qur'an. Ibn Ḥajar al-Haythamī and others considered it a major sin to forget what one has memorized of the Qur'an.

It is prohibited to derive rulings from either the Qur'an or the hadith unless one has fulfilled the prerequisites of an independent jurist (*mujtahid*) or has studied what the rightly-guided scholars have said about a particular verse or hadith.

We are commanded to remain humble in the presence of the Book and the hadith and maintain in our hearts the following three Qur'anic injunctions:

- seek refuge in Allah from Satan before we read anything from the Qur'an;
- do not be forward (with our own understanding) in the presence of Allah (His Book) and His Messenger ﷺ (the Sunnah); and
- ask the people of remembrance (*ahl al-dhikr*) if we do not know.

REMEMBRANCE OF ALLAH

We must be committed to a serious practice of remembrance of Allah (*dhikr*) and be actively engaged in purifying and preparing our hearts for the inevitable meeting with our Lord. *Dhikr* has a profound effect on the heart and should not be underestimated; it must be done regularly, even in small amounts. A little that is constant is better than a lot without consistency.

The minimum *dhikr* should include a portion of the Qur'an every day and the prayers and orations that the Prophet ﷺ was known to recite in the mornings and in the evenings.

Any litany (*wird*) used should be taken from the confirmed prayers of the Prophet ﷺ. We should also incorporate the prayers of our Prophet ﷺ for acts that we perform throughout the day. These are profound tools for keeping a state of presence and connectedness with our Lord and with the Prophet ﷺ.

The greatest remembrance of Allah is to obey His injunctions and avoid what is prohibited. The more one remembers Allah, the easier it becomes to follow His injunctions. Following the Sunnah is our least common denominator. Qadi Abū Bakr said:

> Concern yourself with the appropriate supplications and litanies in their respective times and places and use only the sound transmissions concerning those matters. Do not adopt litanies that do not have a strong foundation. Indeed, if Satan is unable to occupy you with other than the remembrance of Allah, then he will attempt to convince you to use formulas that are innovations and have no foundation.[7]

We should all give some portion of the night, or at least some time after the dawn prayer, to our Lord as an extra show of gratitude. The Prophet ﷺ is our example, and he spent many a night in prayer; when asked about it, he said, "Should I not be a grateful servant?"[8]

COMMANDING GOOD AND FORBIDDING EVIL

We are obliged to learn the rules of commanding good and forbidding evil before attempting to do so, as we may not realize all of the necessary ramifications of any given circumstance. These rules can be found in Imam al-Ghazzālī's *Revival of the Religious Sciences* and have been translated by Shaykh Nuh Keller in *The Reliance of the Traveler.*[9]

EMPATHY

The most beneficial spiritual practice for our hearts is to avoid judging and criticizing people and to cultivate empathy and compassion in our hearts for the creation of Allah. To do this, it helps to remember the narration of the Prophet Jesus ﷺ, found in the *Muwaṭṭa'* of Imam Mālik, which says:

> Mālik related to me [Yaḥyā b. Yaḥyā] that he heard that ʿĪsā Ibn Maryam [Jesus, the son of Mary] ﷺ used to say, "Do not sit in a gathering without the mention of Allah, for you will harden your hearts. A hard heart is far from Allah, but you do not know. Do not look at the wrong actions of people as if you were lords, but rather look at your own wrong actions as if you were slaves. Some people are afflicted by wrong actions and others are protected from them. Have mercy on those who are afflicted, and show gratitude for His protection."[10]

SUPPLICATION

Supplication (*duʿā'*) is another profound practice: pray every day for our afflicted brothers and sisters throughout the world, especially defenseless women and children. May Allah give us from His presence a protector who is victorious. The state of the community of Muslims is at a low ebb in history, but we believe in the promises of our Prophet ﷺ concerning its rectification in the latter days, and we should hope and pray for the day when the community's prosperity returns and the believers are united and protected.

PHYSICAL HEALTH

We should all make it a practice to care for our physical health and hygiene. The Prophet ﷺ said, "Surely your body has a right over you."[11] We should exercise regularly and remove harmful foods from our diets. We are called to be witnesses over humanity in all things. The Prophet ﷺ also said, "A strong believer is better and more beloved to Allah than a weak believer, and in each there is good."[12] Martial arts, especially self-defense and archery, are ancient prophetic practices and effective ways of keeping fit and sharp. Playing sports is useful; it teaches people to work together and cooperate, in addition to providing healthy competition tempered by good-sportsmanship. We know that the Prophet ﷺ raced on foot, on horse, and on camel, and lived an active and vigorous physical life. His stomach was described as being strong and flat even in his later years.

Cleanliness is a characteristic of Islam. Both internal and external cleanliness are important aspects of the prophetic practice. Good external hygiene is achieved by means of bathing, grooming, and wearing clean clothes as well as healthful vigilance in keeping free from impurities. Houses and cars should be maintained inside and out; the Prophet ﷺ said, "Clean your yards."[13] One of the greatest benefits of cleanliness is that it invites the love of Allah. Allah says in the Qur'an:

إِنَّ ٱللَّهَ يُحِبُّ ٱلتَّوَّٰبِينَ وَيُحِبُّ ٱلْمُتَطَهِّرِينَ

Verily, Allah loves those who turn to Him constantly,
and He loves those who keep themselves clean. (2:222)

In *The Medicine of the Prophet,* Imam Ibn Qayyim al-Jawziyyah said that what we eat affects our behavior, and Allah has prohibited the flesh of predators and omnivores so that we do not become like them. We should avoid, to the best of our ability, processed foods and feed our families wholesome, chemical-free natural foods prepared at home with the remembrance of Allah. The blessing found in wholesome food will more than compensate for its additional cost.

COMMITMENT

We should renew our commitment to the religion of Allah and His Messenger ﷺ every day of our lives. Our sole purpose in living should be for Allah's sake. Renewing this pledge of one's life to Allah and then to His Messenger ﷺ is an important daily reminder of why we are here and how we should act. The only way we can truly be witnesses to humanity is to live our truth. This takes great effort, but its rewards are nothing less than guidance and success in this world, and then forgiveness and triumph in the next.

TIME

We should all be committed to utilizing our time as wisely and productively as possible. To squander time or allow the theft of this precious gift of time is a sin, the reality of which will only be clear in the next life. Each moment is priceless and, once gone, can never be replaced. Wasting time is a perennial problem; the first-century stoic, Seneca said, "The problem is not that we have such a short space of time, but that we waste so much of it. Life is long enough, and it has been given in sufficiently generous measure to allow the accomplishment of the very greatest things if the whole of it is well-invested." But modern life is a concerted conspiracy to deprive us of our precious time. The tragedy is that most of us are willful co-conspirators. We fill our lives with distractions and time-consuming trivialities like mindless entertainment and countless other activities that produce little or no benefit. Perhaps the greatest thieves of time in our age are the television and the Internet. Trivial conversations on phones and social media are a modern form of vain talk. The Qur'an says the believers are *those who avoid vain talk* (23:3). Moreover, the Prophet ﷺ informed us that Allah loathes "he said, she said" (*qīla wa qāl*) conversations.

Our lives are akin to an hourglass, and each grain of time that passes takes us one instant closer to our inevitable meeting with Allah. Reflection on death in a serious and constant way is one of the greatest catalysts for change. When terminally ill people realize they are dying, they undergo a profound transformation and make peace with many of the people they had hurt and had bad feelings toward when they were "well."

We are all terminally ill, and prisoners on time's death row. It is only a matter of time before the executioner, the angel of death, makes his call. We should reflect on the sound hadith, "Consider yourselves already people of the grave."[14]

While a governor's pardon is rare in this world, Allah's pardon is very much a possibility in the next. Hope of a divine pardon is reason enough for good behavior while in prison, as reprieves are generally given to model prisoners. The Prophet ﷺ said, "This world is a prison for the believer and a [false] paradise for the unbeliever."[15] He also said, "There are two blessings most people are cheated out of: good health and free time."[16] Our very souls are the greatest thieves, robbing us of our good health and free time.

ATTITUDE

We were created to know, love, and serve our Lord and to honor our parents, and our faith is not complete until we want for humanity what we want for ourselves. Let us aspire to be people whom our Prophet ﷺ will be proud of on the Day he is given the banner of praise (*liwa' al-*

ḥamd). We should never settle for anything less than excellence in our lives and for this religion. *Iḥsān* (virtuous excellence) in everything is the acme of our faith. We should set out to perfect, to the best of our ability, our knowledge of Allah, our love of Allah and His Prophet ﷺ, and our service to His precious gift to us, Islam. The Prophet ﷺ also said, "Surely, Allah has prescribed excellence in all things."[17]

وَإِنَّ ٱللَّهَ لَمَعَ ٱلْمُحْسِنِينَ

Allah is with the people of excellence. (29:69)

DEVOTION

We should commit to realizing *taqwā* within our lifetimes, actively and consciously, and devote ourselves more to it than others devote to mastering the many trivialities this life offers.

وَمِنَ ٱلنَّاسِ مَن يَتَّخِذُ مِن دُونِ ٱللَّهِ أَندَادًا يُحِبُّونَهُمْ كَحُبِّ ٱللَّهِ ۖ
وَٱلَّذِينَ ءَامَنُوٓا۟ أَشَدُّ حُبًّا لِّلَّهِ ۗ

Among humanity are those who take idols beside Allah. They love them with the same love [one should have for] Allah. But those who believe love Allah even more. (2:165)

Realizing *taqwā* during our lives is possible; there is no injunction in the Qur'an that cannot be achieved by those it is incumbent upon. The purpose of all the wondrous signs that Allah has placed in us (life, ability, will, speech, sight, hearing, and knowing) will be realized:

وَفِىٓ أَنفُسِكُمْ ۚ أَفَلَا تُبْصِرُونَ

In yourselves, do you not see? (51:21)

ENDNOTES

1. *Tajwīd* must be taken from a qualified teacher. By the grace of Allah, there are many Muslims in most communities who have learned the rules of Qur'anic recitation.
2. According to one of our teachers, the noble scholar Shaykh Hishām

al-Burhānī, "The weakness of the chain in the hadith of the lesser and greater struggle does not diminish the truth of the statement by the consensus of the rightly-guided scholars." There are also texts whose meaning affirms the existence of the struggle against the soul. For example, Allah says, *Those who struggle in Our way* (jāhada fīnā), *We will guide them in Our paths* (29:69). Imam al-Qurṭubī and others say that the struggle mentioned in this verse includes that undertaken against one's very soul.

3. See Qur'an, 49:11.
4. Imam Mālik b. Anas, al-Muwaṭṭa', trans. Aisha Bewley and Yaᶜqub Johnson (Cambridge: Diwan Press, 1982), p.438.
5. Imam Abū ᶜAbd Allāh Muḥammad b. Yazīd b. Mājah, Sunan Ibn Mājah: Kitāb al-nikāḥ (n.p.: Maṭbaᶜat Dār Iḥyā' al-Kutub al-ᶜArabiyyah, n.d.), 1:50.
6. Imam Abū ᶜĪsā Muḥammad b. ᶜĪsā al-Tirmidhī, Jāmiᶜ al-Tirmidhī (Riyadh: Dār al-Salām, 1420/1999) p.467, no.2029.
7. Qadi Abū Bakr b. al-ᶜArabī, Qānūn al-ta'wīl (Beirut: Dār al-Gharb al-Islāmī, n.d.), p.392.
8. Ṣaḥīḥ al-Bukhārī, pp.879–880, no.4837.
9. Aḥmad b. Naqīb al-Miṣrī, Reliance of the Traveler, trans. Nuh Ha Mim Keller (Beltsville, MD: Amana Publications, 1997), pp.713–725.
10. Imam Mālik, al-Muwaṭṭa', pp. 490–491. The translation here is slightly altered from the original.
11. Ṣaḥīḥ al-Bukhārī, p. 338, no. 1975.
12. Ṣaḥīḥ Muslim, p. 1130, no. 2664.
13. Historically, the Europeans were not clean, and much of their present-day cleanliness is a result of the influence of Islam on Europe. Unfortunately, today it is the Muslims who often live in squalor and become a tribulation for those outside of Islam. Our Lord, do not make us a tribulation for those who reject You (Qur'an, 60:5).
14. Jāmiᶜ al-Tirmidhī, p.534, no.2333.
15. Ibid., p. 532, no. 2324.
16. Ṣaḥīḥ al-Bukhārī, p. 1147, no. 2412.
17. Ṣaḥīḥ Muslim, p. 873, no. 1955

4

Exercises For Attaining *Taqwā*

WHAT FOLLOWS IS an agenda, which is latin for "a set of things to do." It is a series of exercises designed to help achieve *taqwā* practically, through protective vigilance of the eight inroads (*thughrah*) of darkness to the heart. The duration of each exercise is forty days, based on the verse of the Qur'an in which Allah promised to "meet" Moses ﷺ after forty days. This respite of forty days enabled Moses ﷺ to prepare for that august meeting. In his commentary, Imam al-Ṣāwī states that the complete service of the servant toward his Lord and the gifts that result from his Lord are completed in forty days. The meaning of this comes from the following hadith, "The completion of vigilance on the borders (*ribāṭ*) is forty days."[1]

These inroads are at the borders of the heart, and this technique has proven effective for many people. If done for the sake of Allah, it will benefit the one who uses it to achieve *taqwā*.

Read through the eight exercises and look deep within your heart of hearts to determine your areas of weakness. For instance, you may not be disobeying Allah with your feet or private parts. If that is the case, then there is no need to do the exercises corresponding to those areas; however, you should maintain vigilance in continuing to guard them. If you find that you have weakness in the other five inroads, then determine which is the worst. For most, it will be the tongue.

Make the commitment to guard all of these inroads, but take the tongue as your first exercise, and commit to mastering it every day for forty consecutive days. The reason for practicing only one exercise at a time is the tradition of the Prophet ﷺ, "This religion is accommodating, and no one attempts excessive strictness in it without it overwhelming him."[2]

Announce to your friends that you are committing to this path and that you need their help. Allah says,

وَتَعَاوَنُوا۟ عَلَى ٱلْبِرِّ وَٱلتَّقْوَىٰ ۖ وَلَا تَعَاوَنُوا۟ عَلَى ٱلْإِثْمِ وَٱلْعُدْوَٰنِ

Help one another with righteousness and taqwā;
and do not help one another in wrongdoing and aggression. (5:2)

We must take this verse seriously—express a deep desire to better ourselves, and true friends will support us.

Initially, we are shocked to find out that it is very difficult to break bad habits of many years, but rest assured: it is possible. Allah does not ask of us more than we are able to bear. We can conquer these bad habits and destructive tendencies. Many great men and women of the past and present have gone down this road and arrived at its destination. Imam Mālik entitled his book, *al-Muwaṭṭa'* (*The Well-trodden Path*). If others can overcome their bad habits, we can as well and should derive from their examples strength and courage.

Once we have mastered the first exercise, we must be vigilant in maintaining it and move on to the next most troublesome trait. It may be, for instance, the eyes or the ears. We should practice each exercise until we are ready to commit to the next.

In no way should we completely ignore the others while focusing on one. Allah commands us to guard all of our limbs at all times, but in order for us to keep from being overwhelmed, we should focus on one exercise at a time. If we focus on one at a time, it enables us to be more vigilant about the others. Obviously, our bad habits stem from our own heedlessness. Therefore, as we become more conscious of our behavior in one area, we will do so in others as a result.

If Allah wills, we will see the results immediately, but we should take heed, as Satan increases his efforts in proportion to ours. He will work on our hearts and try to instill pride in us for our efforts. He will attempt to make us think we are better than others for struggling with ourselves. We must not succumb to these whispers—and we will hear them!

The path of self-effacement for the sake of Allah demands that we view everyone as better than us. The Muslim should never elevate himself over anyone in creation. Even if we maintain humility, we must remain vigilant because Satan will endeavor to make us feel pleased with being humble. The path to *taqwā* has many pitfalls. According to the Qur'anic narrative, Satan swore an oath regarding this path:

لَأَقْعُدَنَّ لَهُمْ صِرَٰطَكَ ٱلْمُسْتَقِيمَ ۞ ثُمَّ لَءَاتِيَنَّهُم مِّنۢ بَيْنِ أَيْدِيهِمْ وَمِنْ خَلْفِهِمْ وَعَنْ أَيْمَٰنِهِمْ وَعَن شَمَآئِلِهِمْ ۖ وَلَا تَجِدُ أَكْثَرَهُمْ شَٰكِرِينَ

I shall lurk in ambush for them on Your straight path.
Then I shall come upon them from before them and from behind them
and from their right sides and from their left sides,
and You will not find most of them grateful. (7:16–17)

Notice that he says that he will lurk in ambush on the straight path, as he is unconcerned with the wayfarers on a crooked path. Moreover, he does not say that he will come from above or from below. The secret in this is that revelation and guidance come from above, and by maintaining a state of humility and keeping our foreheads to the ground, we open our hearts to the guidance from above. Allah has not given Satan authority over the guidance of the Prophet ﷺ or His humbled servants who follow that guidance.

This is the ancient hero's journey, and success is by Allah; not by deeds but by grace alone is this achieved. We must see our progress as *tawfiq* (providence) from Allah, which means our gratitude must increase as spiritual growth occurs. It cannot be done without effort, but it is not effort through which it is done. Use bifocal vision to see paradoxical truth,[3] and submit to it. Let us keep our eye on the goal ahead. Let us constantly remember our mortality and know that we will be considered among those who reached the goal before us, even if we die before reaching them. This is why we pray,

وَأَلْحِقْنِى بِٱلصَّٰلِحِينَ

Cause me to reach the righteous. (12:101)

EXERCISE 1: GUARDING THE PRAYER

Of all the actions that a Muslim will do in his or her life, none is more important than the five prescribed daily prayers. It is the central pillar that supports the entire edifice of Islam. The Qur'an defines the believers as follows:

ٱلَّذِينَ يُؤْمِنُونَ بِٱلْغَيْبِ وَيُقِيمُونَ ٱلصَّلَوٰةَ وَمِمَّا رَزَقْنَٰهُمْ يُنفِقُونَ

Those who believe in the unseen and establish prayer,
and from what We provide for them, they give out. (2:3)

Thus, prayer is mentioned immediately after belief; it is a believer's expression of gratitude to his Lord for consciousness itself, the gift of life and awareness. A divine tradition (*ḥadīth qudsī*) related by Imam al-Ḥākim, on the authority of ʿĀ'ishah ﷺ states,

> There are five prayers that Allah has ordained for [His] servants. Whoever dutifully undertakes them without belittling the right they embody in any way, he has a covenant with Allah that He will enter him into Paradise.[4]

Commenting on this hadith, Imam al-Munāwī states:

> The use of the definite article in "the prayer" indicates that what is meant is the *complete prayer,* which fulfills the pillars, near integrals (confirmed Sunan), recommended matters, and all the other conditions of the prayer. There is no doubt that the one who fulfills this will be a true believer. He is someone who would avoid the prohibited matters and fulfill his obligations. He would engage his soul in the obedience of his Lord. Indeed, Allah says in His Book that was revealed to His ennobled servant ﷺ, *Surely, prayer prevents anything foul or indecent* [29:45]. Anyone who possesses this state is worthy of being spared from the punishment of Allah and of being given the Garden without any accounting. And Allah knows best.[5]

Allah says in the Qur'an,

إِنَّ ٱلصَّلَوٰةَ كَانَتْ عَلَى ٱلْمُؤْمِنِينَ كِتَـٰبًا مَّوْقُوتًا

Surely, prayer has been prescribed
for the believers at specific times. (4:103)

Allah also says,

وَٱسْتَعِينُوا۟ بِٱلصَّبْرِ وَٱلصَّلَوٰةِ ۚ وَإِنَّهَا لَكَبِيرَةٌ إِلَّا عَلَى ٱلْخَـٰشِعِينَ

Seek assistance with patience and prayer,
and surely it is a difficult matter
except for the believers. (2:45)

It is one of the extraordinary insights of Imam Mālik that the first section of his *Muwaṭṭa'*, which precedes even the section on ritual purity, is on the times of the prayer. It is the times of prayer that obligate purity. Observing the times of prayer is the first thing we do when we wake and the last thing we do before retiring to bed; it is done in the middle of the day and in its decline. It is an unrelenting reminder of to whom we belong, why we are here, and where we are going. Imam Mālik wrote,

> I heard from Nāfiᶜ [who heard] from Ibn ᶜUmar that ᶜUmar b. al-Khaṭṭāb ﷺ wrote to all of his governors saying, "The most important of your affairs in my view is the prayer. Whoever protects it and observes it carefully is protecting his religion, while whoever is negligent about it will be even more negligent about other things."[6]

This is advice from the man whom Satan completely avoided: "If [ᶜUmar] went down a path, Satan would take another route."[7] Surely, remaining in a state of purity and being regular in prayer will keep Satan away from us.

The ritual prayer is the believer's protection and connection with his Lord. The prayer is a science and an art that takes many years of serious and vigilant practice in order to arrive at its true reality. The first and most important matter is to learn its form. This involves studying a valid text from one of the canonical schools of Islam with a teacher who is licensed to teach that section of the rules of *fiqh* (jurisprudence). When seeking a teacher, keep in mind the hadith related by Imam al-Tirmidhī and others: "The great scholar Ibn Sīrīn said, 'Sacred knowledge is the essence of religion. So let each of you examine well whom he takes his knowledge from.'"

The next stage is to be vigilant about ritual purity (*wuḍū'* and *ghusl*) and about the avoidance of urine and any other impurities (*najāsah*). Be sure to study both the section on impurities and the section on purification. According to the great scholar and reviver of the last century, Imam Muḥammad Mawlūd al-Yaᶜqūbī, the rules of prayer should be reviewed every six months in order to keep them fresh.

Finally, let us all heed the advice of the great Moroccan scholar, Shaykh ᶜAbd al-Raḥmān al-Akhḍarī, who says in his text on the prayer,

> The prayer contains a vast spiritual light that radiates in the hearts of those who truly pray, but it is only obtainable by one who has humbly submitted himself. Thus, should you come to

the prayer, empty your heart of the ephemeral world and what it contains, and occupy yourself with vigilant awareness of your Master for whose sake you are praying. Firmly believe that your prayer is humility and abasement for the sake of Allah, Exalted above attribution is He, by means of standing, bowing, and prostrating.

Moreover, it is a form of reverence and magnification of Him by means of saying "*Allāhu akbar,*" "*subḥāna l-lāh,*" and the other general remembrances. Thus, guard your prayer, as it is the greatest of all acts of worship. Do not allow Satan to play with your heart and preoccupy you during your prayers to such an extent that he blinds your heart's eye and deprives you of the pleasure of the spiritual lights of the prayer. Therefore, have constant humility in it, for surely it prevents you from [committing] foulness and misdeeds because of that very humility in it. Seek help from Allah, for surely He is the best of those whose help is sought.[8]

The duration of the exercise for the prayer is forty days. We should stipulate with ourselves that for forty consecutive days, we will pray all five prayers at their respective times without missing one, while fulfilling each prayer's conditions, pillars, near integrals, and recommended acts. If any of the prayers is not prayed on time, then we must start the forty-day period over. The exercise may take a long time to complete, but this is the struggle of the believer, so we should never despair. For a man, this exercise is preferably performed in congregation and preferably in the mosque, but due to the fact that many people in Western countries do not live near a mosque, this is not always an option. If one can pray at least the dawn prayer and the night prayer in a mosque, then the reward is greater. A family is counted as a congregation. Therefore, it is important for a husband, wife, and children who are seven years of age and older to pray together in the house if congregational prayers are not held in your area.

The Prophet Muḥammad ﷺ said, "If people knew what was in the congregational prayer, they would attend it even if it meant they crawled."[9] The early companions also said that if someone did not attend prayers in the mosque regularly without a valid excuse, they considered him to be a hypocrite. A sure sign of hypocrites is that when the prayer time comes in, they are lazy and procrastinate until the time is almost out:

وَإِذَا قَامُوٓاْ إِلَى ٱلصَّلَوٰةِ قَامُواْ كُسَالَىٰ

If they get up to pray, they do so slothfully. (4:142)

The three prayers that require special vigilance are the dawn (*ṣubḥ*), midday (*ʿaṣr*), and the sunset (*maghrib*) prayers. Some people miss the dawn prayer out of laziness or too much activity into the early hours of the morning. It is Sunnah to retire at night after the night prayer is performed, and there is great wisdom in that practice, as in all of the prophetic traditions. The midday prayer is probably the "middle prayer" that the Qur'an warns us of when Allah says,

حَـٰفِظُواْ عَلَى ٱلصَّلَوَٰتِ وَٱلصَّلَوٰةِ ٱلْوُسْطَىٰ

Be vigilant about your prayers
and particularly of the middle prayer. (2:238)

Imam Mālik, following the opinions of ʿAlī ﵁ and Ibn ʿAbbās ﵄, considered the middle prayer to be the dawn prayer. The hadith in al-Bukhārī mentions the midday prayer as the middle prayer, and, in some ways, the middle prayer is like the Night of Power—it is hidden within the prayers, so we should be vigilant about all of them. The sunset prayer has a very short time in which it must be performed, whereas the post-meridian prayer and the night prayer have longer valid time frames and are more flexible for peoples' schedules, should people need to delay them.

Upon faltering in an exercise, we need to levy a self-imposed penalty to discipline the *nafs*, such as spending in charity or fasting. It is also better to do this with others as a way of enjoining each other to righteousness and *taqwā*.

Once we are performing the five obligatory prayers with regularity, then it is certainly worth our efforts to begin increasing extra prayers—especially the late-night prayers (*tahajjud*). Late-night prayer is one of the defining qualities of a *ṣāliḥ* (righteous) person, also called a *walī* (friend of Allah). Regarding late-night prayers, Fuḍayl b. ʿIyyāḍ said that if a man was unable to do them, it was due to his wrong actions during the day. May Allah make us befitting to stand before Him, here and in the hereafter.

EXERCISE 2: GUARDING THE TONGUE

Qadi Abū Bakr says, "Guard your tongue, and protect it from lying, and realize that it expresses your inward state. It reveals to you the depth of your knowledge and your practice."

The tongue has only one noble quality, and that is truthfulness. It has over twenty destructive qualities, but their sources are rooted in the following four:

- lying;
- backbiting;
- argumentation; and
- engaging in what does not concern you.

If you are able to overcome them, then all the others are removed with ease. In order for us to remove these qualities that lead people to destruction, we must exert great effort and struggle (*mujāhadah*).

The following is an exercise designed to help eliminate these qualities that have become daily habits for far too many among us and, in fact, if we persist in them, are counted as enormities with Allah. Imam Mālik stated, "Truly a man utters words to which he attaches no importance, and by them he falls into the Hellfire (*jahannam*)."[10]

This exercise includes the following steps:

- Commit every day, for forty days, to leave the aforementioned four habits. Each morning, make a vow to Allah, "I vow to not lie, backbite, argue, or speak in matters of no concern to me for this entire day." This is the condition phase (*mushāraṭah*).
- Throughout the day, be vigilant in observing and noting the times when you did not fulfill the condition. This is guarding the condition (*murābaṭah*).
- At the end of the day, account for your deeds (*muḥāsabah*). If you succeed, then say, "O Allah, I can honestly say I did not commit any of these offences today." If, on the other hand, you did not fulfill your vow, then go back to day one, and start over. Ask for forgiveness and strength in fulfilling it for the next day, and give in charity, fast, or impose some other type of disciplinary measure to benefit your soul.

We should remind ourselves that our eternal life and felicity in it is largely dependent upon whether our tongues are in submission to the will of Allah. Hence, we must take this seriously. Do this practice with your brothers and sisters that you spend time with, and encourage each other to be vigilant.

This practice requires significant discipline and effort; Allah encouraged us to persevere with this verse:

وَٱلَّذِينَ جَٰهَدُوا۟ فِينَا لَنَهْدِيَنَّهُمْ سُبُلَنَا ۚ وَإِنَّ ٱللَّهَ لَمَعَ ٱلْمُحْسِنِينَ

Those who struggle in Our way, We guide them in Our paths, and Allah is with the people of excellence. (29:69)

This practice will change our lives and our outlooks and will contribute to the unity of our community, as most of our trouble, if not all of it, is reaped from the harvest of our tongues.

Once forty consecutive days have been completed, we have habituated ourselves to uprightness, and Allah promises two things for our efforts: He will rectify our affairs in this world, and He will forgive our transgressions in the next. Allah says,

يَٰٓأَيُّهَا ٱلَّذِينَ ءَامَنُوا۟ ٱتَّقُوا۟ ٱللَّهَ وَقُولُوا۟ قَوْلًا سَدِيدًا ۞

يُصْلِحْ لَكُمْ أَعْمَٰلَكُمْ وَيَغْفِرْ لَكُمْ ذُنُوبَكُمْ ۗ

O you who believe, have taqwā, and speak with uprightness; He will rectify your actions, and He will forgive your wrongs. (33:70–71)

Once we have fulfilled the exercise successfully, what remains is vigilant observance (*murāqabah*) in order to prevent a relapse. We must be firm with others and make clear to them that we do not want to listen to prohibited speech. This may result in the loss of a friend who is not willing to change.

Finally, we should keep in mind that writing falls into these categories, and that the Internet is infested with lies, slander, argumentation, and engagement in matters of no concern. Therefore, we need to include writing, in addition to speech, in the vow.

EXERCISE 3: GUARDING THE EYES

Allah says in the Qur'an,

قُل لِّلْمُؤْمِنِينَ يَغُضُّوا۟ مِنْ أَبْصَـٰرِهِمْ وَيَحْفَظُوا۟ فُرُوجَهُمْ ۚ ذَٰلِكَ أَزْكَىٰ لَهُمْ ۗ إِنَّ ٱللَّهَ خَبِيرٌۢ بِمَا يَصْنَعُونَ ۞ وَقُل لِّلْمُؤْمِنَـٰتِ يَغْضُضْنَ مِنْ أَبْصَـٰرِهِنَّ وَيَحْفَظْنَ فُرُوجَهُنَّ

Tell the believing men to lower their gaze and guard their modesty ... and tell the believing women to lower their gaze and guard their modesty. (24:30–31)

The scholars differ about the meaning and implication of this verse, but generally what is prohibited is to look at anything that is deemed nakedness in sacred law, though not all the scholars agree on what constitutes "nakedness." For the majority of scholars, this includes for a man the entire body of a woman with the exception of her face and hands, and for another man what is between the navel and knees.[11]

However, the scholars consider anything from which we derive sexual pleasure prohibited to look at unless it is of our lawful spouse. For this reason, the body of a man is prohibited for a woman to look at if it arouses her carnal instincts. Similarly, for a man, looking at the face and hands of a woman is also prohibited if that arouses his carnal instincts.

The first glance is not written against a person. However, if one derives pleasure and does not avert one's glance, or if one follows it with a second glance, then it is considered a minor sin. Ibn al-Qaṭṭān said, "There is a consensus that the eye is not connected to any enormity, but it is the quickest inroad to the destruction of the heart."[12]

We must also guard ourselves against sensory images that have corrupting influences on the heart. Much of what is on television and around us in terms of billboards and images is actually detrimental to our hearts. We should avert our gaze from these corrupting influences also.

The exercise for the eyes is to make a commitment to Allah every morning for forty continuous days to not look at anything prohibited. Throughout the day, be vigilant and keep in mind that averting the glance is an essential element in the practice of protecting the eyes and thereby the heart. In other words, you will see things that are prohibited, but count the day as successful if you averted your glance from them.

In our culture, we have what could be termed an "in your face" bombardment of images and ads, as well as an immodest world of fashion and apparel. It is thus extremely important with this exercise that we not become neurotic about our situations. Lowering the gaze is a profound spiritual practice in any time and place and can be done with dignity and a naturalness that does not lead to obsessive behaviors that may be detrimental and lead to social pathology.

Mark each day, and go back to day one if you fail. Use some punitive measure to discipline yourself.

EXERCISE 4: GUARDING THE EARS

Allah says,

إِنَّ ٱلسَّمْعَ وَٱلْبَصَرَ وَٱلْفُؤَادَ كُلُّ أُوْلَٰٓئِكَ كَانَ عَنْهُ مَسْـُٔولًا

Surely the hearing, the sight, and the heart,
all of those, man is responsible for. (17:36)

Allah says, regarding believers,

وَإِذَا سَمِعُوا۟ ٱللَّغْوَ أَعْرَضُوا۟ عَنْهُ

When they hear empty talk, they turn away from it. (28:55)

One hadith states, "The listener is one of the backbiters."[13] The ears, unlike the eyes, are more difficult to guard because there is no natural plug for the ears as there is with the lids of the eyes. Moreover, we cannot avert our hearing with as much ease as we can our eyes.

Imam Mālik said, "Do not give your ear to someone whose heart is deviant because you do not know what will become attached to it."[14] The ear is a direct inroad to the heart, and through it, meanings enter into the understanding.

Commit to breaking the bad habits associated with the ears, as follows:

- turn away from vain talk, as it is an attribute of those with no faith, according to the Qur'an;
- do not listen to lies, slander, calumny, backbiting, mockery, or any other prohibited deed of the tongue;
- change the subject if people begin to speak ill of someone. If they refuse, explain to them what you are trying to do and that what they are saying is probably backbiting; and
- avoid most television programming, which often exposes believers to forbidden speech and images. Most broadcast television should be avoided. Educational visual media or halal recreational media should be purposeful and viewed within reasonable time limits. Visual media involves both the eyes and ears, and one should keep in mind both are immense sacred trusts given to humanity to protect from harm and utilize for benefit.

Again, do the exercise for forty days. If you fail to fulfill your commitment, start back at day one until you have accomplished forty consecutive days.

In all of these exercises, we should always work on eliminating the prohibited (*haram*) first and foremost. Discouraged matters (*makrūh*)[15] or matters on which the sacred law is neutral (*mubāḥ*) can be worked on later. No punishment is threatened for actions that are discouraged or merely permitted. Once we have successfully eliminated the prohibited, we can work on removing discouraged things from our lives. For those with high spiritual aspirations, work on eliminating purposeless activity from life.

The scholars consider profane music impermissible and differ concerning other types. Our culture, again, is filled with music, and it permeates virtually every aspect of life. We should use as much of our free time as possible for beneficial activities, especially performing or listening to Qur'an recitation as well as educational lectures. For recreation, we should limit ourselves to permissible activities, which include poetry and song.[16] We should try to avoid doubtful and clearly prohibited environments. If unavoidable, then do not count that as a breach of your commitment. Absolute necessities temporarily legitimize the unlawful.

EXERCISE 5: GUARDING THE STOMACH

Guarding the stomach is perhaps the most important of the exercises. Some may even want to begin with this exercise, particularly those who are eating foods that are clearly prohibited, such as those produced or purchased with unlawful income.

It is an obligation according to the Qur'an, Sunnah, and scholarly consensus to guard what goes into our stomachs. Allah says,

يَـٰٓأَيُّهَا ٱلنَّاسُ كُلُوا۟ مِمَّا فِى ٱلْأَرْضِ حَلَـٰلًا طَيِّبًا

O you who believe, eat from the earth
what is permissible and pure. (2:168)

Again, Allah says,

يَـٰٓأَيُّهَا ٱلَّذِينَ ءَامَنُوا۟ كُلُوا۟ مِن طَيِّبَـٰتِ مَا رَزَقْنَـٰكُمْ

O you who believe, eat from the pure things
that We provided for you. (2:172)

And again, Allah says,

يَـٰٓأَيُّهَا ٱلرُّسُلُ كُلُوا۟ مِنَ ٱلطَّيِّبَـٰتِ وَٱعْمَلُوا۟ صَـٰلِحًا

O Messengers, eat from the pure things,
and do righteous deeds. (23:51)

The commentators say that there is a direct relation between doing righteous works and eating pure foods. In this context, purity means that both the food itself and its source are pure.

Ibn ʿAbbās ﷺ said, "Allah has commanded the believers to do the same thing that He has commanded the Messengers [in the aforementioned verse]. He commanded them to perform righteous deeds after commanding them to eat pure foods as a reminder that one does not derive benefit from actions until one has rectified one's livelihood and provision."[17]

Sīdī Aḥmad Zarrūq said, "Eat what you will, but know that you will act accordingly."[18] One hadith clearly states, "Flesh that has been nourished with the prohibited is more worthy of the Fire."[19]

During this exercise, one should focus on removing any prohibited food substances or sources. As for meat of the People of the Book, it is permissible by consensus. However, there are many questionable aspects and serious health concerns associated with modern-day meat production. Most store-bought meat, and even some meat advertised as halal, comes from animals that are genetically-engineered, fed by-products of other animals, injected with growth hormones and antibiotics, and confined to cages and cramped pens inside feedlots and inhumane "factories." Indeed, one should avoid many of the sources of meat today.[20]

Eating less is also an important part of this exercise. Begin by avoiding excess on a regular basis, as Allah commands,

يَـٰبَنِىٓ ءَادَمَ خُذُوا۟ زِينَتَكُمْ عِندَ كُلِّ مَسْجِدٍ وَكُلُوا۟ وَٱشْرَبُوا۟ وَلَا
تُسْرِفُوٓا۟ ۚ إِنَّهُۥ لَا يُحِبُّ ٱلْمُسْرِفِينَ

O children of Adam take your adornment to every mosque. Eat and drink but not to excess. Surely Allah loves not the excessive. (7:31)

Learning to control the appetite is one of the most powerful means of controlling the self and achieving *taqwā*, which is why Allah says about fasting,

يَـٰٓأَيُّهَا ٱلَّذِينَ ءَامَنُوا۟ كُتِبَ عَلَيْكُمُ ٱلصِّيَامُ كَمَا كُتِبَ عَلَى ٱلَّذِينَ
مِن قَبْلِكُمْ لَعَلَّكُمْ تَتَّقُونَ

O you who believe, fasting has been prescribed for you as it was prescribed for those before you, in order to achieve taqwā. (2:183)

Fasting is an excellent discipline, and fasting at least three days per month from dawn to sunset when the moon is full is a prophetic practice. Fasting on Mondays and Thursdays is also a prophetic practice.

Finally, the greatest rule here is the one provided by the Messenger of Allah ﷺ who said, "Leave what gives you doubt for what does not give you doubt."[21] Apply this principle in the other exercises as well.

Note: There is no special time consideration for the stomach in terms of guarding it from the prohibited. The skin also must be protected by wearing only what is permissible and pure.

EXERCISE 6: GUARDING THE PRIVATE PARTS

Guarding the private parts simply entails avoiding places of temptation and possible harm. One should never, under any circumstances, be alone with someone of the opposite sex who is not directly a legal relation, such as one's spouse or a direct relative (mother, father, sibling, aunt, uncle, grandparent, and others).

Allah says of the believers that they

وَٱلَّذِينَ هُمۡ لِفُرُوجِهِمۡ حَٰفِظُونَ * إِلَّا عَلَىٰٓ أَزۡوَٰجِهِمۡ

... protect their private parts,
except with their spouses. (23:5–6)

Likewise, Allah says,

وَلَا تَقۡرَبُواْ ٱلزِّنَىٰٓۖ إِنَّهُۥ كَانَ فَٰحِشَةٗ وَسَآءَ سَبِيلٗا

Do not even enter into proximity of fornication or perversion,
for it is foul and leads to a bad path. (17:32)

For the believer, this should be the easiest of the exercises, if he or she follows the simple rule of never being alone with someone of the oppposite sex who is not directly related to him or her. The Prophet ﷺ said, "Whoever guards for me his tongue and private parts, I guarantee him a place in the Garden."[22]

Regarding homosexual acts, these are condemned by sacred law and are considered enormities that require repentance. If Muslims are tried with such impulses, they are obliged to struggle with themselves and avoid being in situations that can lead to temptation or compromise. A person engaged in such an effort should see it as a form of spiritual struggle, for which he or she will receive a great reward in the hereafter and spiritual elevation in this world. Many peoples throughout history have abstained entirely from sexual relations, and it is certainly within human capacity for those with unsavory desires to refrain from them for the sake of their Lord and Sustainer.

As for masturbation, opinions vary from prohibition to permissibility, but all are in agreement that it is not a dignified practice. If one is engaged in its practice, one should commit to stopping. If someone is single and has overwhelming sexual impulses that are obstructing his or her well-being, marriage is an obligation. If, for whatever reasons, marriage is not an option, and the fear of committing fornication is great, then masturbation is better than fornication. Imam Aḥmad considers it akin to medicinal cupping, which removes blocked fluids, but stipulates that it not be habitual nor involve any lustful fantasizing.[23]

One should also guard one's nakedness and avoid any display of what is prohibited for others to see. This means Muslim women should make a strong commitment to covering themselves accordingly, and men should also dress modestly. Both men and women should avoid wearing tight-fitting or revealing clothing.

Again, do this exercise like the others, and maintain vigilance—sexual appetite is one of Satan's greatest weapons. If someone has committed a grave wrong, he or she needs to make sincere repentance and commit to never doing it again. If that wrong involves compromising the right of another person, he or she should restore that right if possible.

EXERCISE 7: GUARDING THE HANDS

The blessed Messenger of Allah ﷺ said, "The Muslim is one from whose tongue and hands other Muslims are safe."[24] This means guarding the hands against stealing from or harming any part of Allah's creation without just cause.

According to the Qur'an, the hands will bear witness against the Children of Adam. Hands are one of the greatest of Allah's gifts and distinguish us from other animals because we not only have an opposable thumb but dexterous hands that enable us to manufacture things (literally "make with hands").

We should never raise our hands to anyone, Muslim or non-Muslim, unless in self-defense or a legitimate struggle for the defense of a country; if living in a Muslim country, one may fight only when a jihad is declared by legitimate state authority and does not involve any vigilantism, which is prohibited by consensus. Even in war, Muslims are prohibited from assaulting or killing women, children, old people, and noncombatants. Furthermore, we should certainly not use our hands to sow any corruption in the earth.

Shaking hands with someone of the opposite sex is generally regarded as prohibited based upon the verse which commands us to lower the gaze (as touch is more arousing than sight), and certain sound hadith warn specifically against shaking hands with members of the opposite sex. Some scholars, however, interpreted those to mean when attraction is present, but these are weak opinions. It is a problem in Western lands, as Muslim men are often seen as misogynistic, and their refusal to shake a woman's hand innocently offered in friendship or in a professional capacity can strengthen this perception. Orthodox Jews are also prohibited from shaking hands with members of the opposite sex and adhere strictly to that practice even in the United States. If one resolves not to shake hands, it is important to explain the reason to those present who might misconstrue the act as an insult. This is a problem even some of the great scholars of this time grapple with.

EXERCISE 8: GUARDING THE FEET

The feet are treated the same as the hands. Our feet are our means of mobility, and therefore we should consider driving or traveling by any means as actions of the feet. We should apply this standard to all endeavors that we undertake. Most deeds are permissible; little is prohibited. We are obliged to learn whatever is prohibited and then avoid those actions.

When we set out to a place, we should recite the prayer of the Prophet Muḥammad ﷺ:

اللَّهُمَّ إِنِّي أعُوذُ بِكَ أَن أضِلَّ أو أُضَلّ ، أو أَزِلَّ أو أُزَلَّ ، أو أظْلِمَ أو أُظْلَمَ ،
أو أجْهَلَ أو يُجْهَلَ عَلَيَّ□

O Allah, I seek refuge in You that I should go astray or lead others astray, that I should trip or trip up others, that I should oppress or be oppressed, or that I should show ignorance or be the brunt of ignorance.[25]

We should always ask ourselves why we are going somewhere and remember that the prophetic tradition teaches us to avoid places that can cast doubt upon one's character.

SUMMARY

If our prayer and the eight aforementioned inroads to wrong actions are guarded, we are actually guarding our hearts, as the heart is a city, and these are its borders. Light and dark forces wage war for our heart, and just as night turns into day and day turns into night, our war with our enemies is one with alternating success (*sijāl*).

We must not despair when we lapse and show weakness. Faltering keeps us humble before our peers and our Lord. Do not give up this struggle, as there is no other as worthy of our efforts. Take this seriously, and remember that *taqwā* is the key to every good in this life and the next, and it is a reality within our reach.

Finally, some of our scholars have said that all of Islam revolves around the following four hadiths. God willing, if we take them seriously and practice them, we will be people of *taqwā*.

- The permissible is clear and the prohibited is clear, and between them are grey areas; not many people know their rulings. So, whoever protects himself from them has kept his religion sound and free of blemish. However, whoever falls into them has fallen into the prohibited.[26] His likeness is that of a shepherd who takes his flock to graze near a king's sanctuary, and due to his proximity to it, he inevitably falls into it. Surely, every king has a sanctuary, and surely the sanctuary of Allah on His earth lies in avoiding those things He has prohibited. Surely, there is a lump of flesh in the body—if it is sound, the whole body is sound, and if it is corrupt, the whole body is corrupt. Is it not the heart?[27]
- Abandon the world, and Allah will love you; and abandon what people have, and people will love you.[28]
- From the excellence of a person's Islam is that he leaves what does not concern him.[29]
- Surely, actions are [judged] by intentions, and everyone has what he has intended.[30]

If we simply take these four hadiths to heart and base our lives upon them, we will indeed have success. May Allah forgive us for words without deeds and not make our religion a proof against us on the Day of Recompense when debts fall due.

ENDNOTES

1. Aḥmad al-Ṣāwī, *Tafsīr al-Ṣāwī ʿalā al-Jalalayn* (Cairo: Dār Iḥyā' al-Kutub al-ʿArabiyyah), 1:51. The hadith is narrated by Imam Ṭabarānī and is weak according to Imam Suyūṭī in *al-Jāmiʿ al-ṣaghīr.* However, the verse and its commentary strengthen the meaning. Also, given that it is an exercise intended to help one fulfill an obligation, it is not an innovation but is similar to using an alarm clock to wake from sleep for prayer. The Jamāʿat al-Tablīgh derive the mission (*khurūj*) of forty days from this. A habit can be firmly established in forty days, and according to the wisdom of the early people, "Whoever lives with a people for forty days becomes one of them."
2. Imam Aḥmad b. al-Ḥusayn al-Bayhaqī, *al-Sunan al-kubrā* (Beirut: Dār al-Kutub al-ʿIlmiyyah, 1994), 3:27, no. 4741.
3. In reality, this is not a paradox but rather an antinomy, and its seeming contradiction can only be resolved by moving to a higher level of understanding. May Allah open our hearts to the subtle knowledge of this religion.
4. Imam Abū ʿAbd al-Raḥmān Aḥmad b. Shuʿayb al-Nasā'ī, *Sunan al-Nasā'ī* (Riyadh: Dār al-Salām, 1420/1999), pp.63–64, no.46.
5. ʿAbd al-Ra'ūf al-Munāwī, *al-Ithāfat al-saniyyah bi al-aḥādīth al-qudsiyyah* (Beirut: Dār al-Maʿrifah, n.d.), p. 37.
6. Imam Mālik, *al-Muwaṭṭa',* 1:1, no. 6.
7. *Ṣaḥīḥ al-Bukhārī,* 4:54, no. 515.
8. ʿAbd al-Raḥmān al-Akhḍarī, *Matn al-Akhḍarī,* trans. Hamza Yusuf, unpublished.
9. Imam Zakī al-Dīn al-Mundhirī, *al-Targhib wa al-tarhīb* (Cairo: Dār al-Ḥadīth, 1987/1407), 1:263.
10. Imam Mālik, *al-Muwaṭṭa',* p. 490. The translation here differs slightly from the original.
11. The Shāfiʿī and Ḥanbalī schools consider a woman's face to be from her nakedness, and this is a valid opinion but cannot be imposed on others who follow the more lenient position of the Mālikī and Ḥanafī schools. All of these schools agree that anyone who is "attractive" should not be looked at for pleasure because this is deriving sensual pleasure (*istimtāʿ*) and is only permissible after a valid contract of marriage has been agreed upon. Lowering the gaze is not necessary for direct relatives of the opposite sex due to the lack of sexual attraction toward them that Allah has instilled in humanity. This requirement is, in fact, due to the high ethics of Islam and its deep respect for a woman's right to privacy and right to not be objectified and made into a source of sexual pleasure for anyone with eyes.

12. Imam Muḥammad b.ʿAlī, *Khamsan farīḍah* (Nigeria: Dār Ifrīqiyyah, n.d.), p.26.

13. Related by Ibn ʿAsākir in his *Tārīkh.* Imam al-Subkī said he could not find a chain for it, but the scholars have said its meaning is true.

14. Imam Muḥammad b. al-Ḥājj, *al-Madkhal* (Beirut: Dār al-Kutub al-ʿIlmiyyah), 2:466.

15. For instance, excessive talking without purpose is *makrūh* because it often leads to prohibited speech, such as speaking ill of others. However, the focus in these exercises should be eliminating, first and foremost, what is prohibited. Follow the stations of *taqwā* mentioned by Ibn Juzayy, as this is the path to success. Attempting to achieve a station by skipping another inevitably leads to failure.

16. More of these recordings are becoming available, and some are very good. There should be more alternatives for our youth who are inundated with music in the dominant culture in which music is very difficult for them to avoid.

17. Muḥammad b. Aḥmad al-Mayyārah al-Fāsī, *Mayyārah al-kabīr* (Egypt: U.A.E. edition, n.d.), 2:253.

18. Aḥmad Zarrūq, *al-Qawāʿid* (Azzam, Tunisia: Maṭābiʿ Muwaḥḥadah, 1987), p.51.

19. Ibid., Ibn ʿAdī, Ibn ʿAsākir, and Imam Ṭabarānī all narrate it.

20. ʿUmar ﷺ did not like to see people eating meat every day. See the chapter in the *Muwaṭṭa'* concerning meat consumption. Also, ʿAlī b. Abī Ṭālib ﷺ said that consistently eating meat made the heart hard. This is certainly true in physical science and has been demonstrated scientifically. We should also trust that it is true in the spiritual understanding as well. Finally, beef consumption is a major contributor to many of the economic problems in the world today. See Jeremy Rifkin, *Beyond Beef* (New York, NY: Plume Publishers, 2003).

21. al-Tirmidhī, p. 572, no. 2518. Imam Aḥmad b. Shuʿayb al-Nasā'ī, *Sunan al-Nasā'ī*, pp. 772–773, no 5714.

22. Ibn Ḥajar al-ʿAsqalānī, *Fatḥ al-Bārī: Sharḥ Ṣaḥīḥ al-Bukhārī* (Damascus: Dār al-Fayḥā', 1997) 11:373, no.6474.

23. Although the Ḥanbalī position permits masturbation, it in no way accepts its habitual practice but rather sees it as a sometimes necessary alternative. The dominant Mālikī position is prohibition, but there is a weaker position that it is *makrūh*, and an even weaker one that deems it permissible. If someone indeed fears committing a grave wrong, then it should be considered the lesser of two evils. And Allah knows best. See al-Mayyārah cited above, p.260. See also Shaykh Muḥammad Aḥmad Kanʿān's *al-Uṣūl al-muʿāshirah al-zawjiyyah* (Beirut: Dār al-Bashā'ir al-Islāmiyyah, n.d.), pp.82–84.

24. Ibn Ḥajar al-ʿAsqalānī, *Fatḥ al-Bārī*, 1:74, no. 10.

25. Imam Ibn Mājah, *Sunan Ibn Mājah* (Riyadh: Dār al-Salām, 1420/1999), p. 556, no.3884.

26. This is a clear proof of the understanding of the Prophet ﷺ for what is now known as "fuzzy logic," in that the continuum is unbroken, and it is impossible to discern precisely when everything is purely permissible or purely prohibited. There will always be matters where the line is blurred, and by engaging in them, you will engage in some part of something prohibited.

27. Ibn Ḥajar al-ʿAsqalānī, *Fatḥ al-Bārī,* 1:167, no.52.

28. Ibn Mājah, p. 598, no. 4102. Imam Muḥammad b. ʿAbd Allāh al-Ḥākim, *al-Mustadrak ʿalā al-ṣaḥīḥayn* (Beirut: Dār al-Kutub al-ʿIlmiyyah, 1990), 4:348, 7873. Al-Iṣfahānī, *Ḥilyat al-awliyā',* 8:41. This hadith is in Imam Nawawī's *Forty Hadith,* and one of the narrators, Khālid b. ʿAmr al-Qurashī, is considered weak by most hadith scholars, although not for his character. It also has other similar transmissions, all of which are weak. The scholars have considered its meaning to be true and thus transmitted it with authority, despite its weakness. It is narrated from the Prophet ﷺ from a successor with a sound chain of transmission.

29. Al-Tirmidhī, p.531, no. 2317. Ibn Mājah, p. 572, no.3976. It is a good hadith (*ḥasan*), but according to Imam Ibn Daqīq al-ʿĪd, it is sound in another transmission. See Ibn Daqīq al-ʿĪd, *Sharḥ al-arbaʿīn al-Nawawīyyah* (Beirut: Dār Ibn Ḥazm, n.d.), p.64.

30. Agreed upon by the two leading authorities on hadith, Imam al-Bukhārī and Imam Muslim.

5

Civic Involvement: An Islamic Imperative

AS WE CONCLUDE THIS AGENDA, let us now direct our attention from our inward state to that of worldly matters. This orientation is not an effort to encourage us to take from the world, as this would contradict much of what was mentioned earlier. Rather, it is part of an effort to improve the world in which we live. We believe that this is an Islamic imperative. Allah says in the Qur'an,

كُنتُمْ خَيْرَ أُمَّةٍ أُخْرِجَتْ لِلنَّاسِ

You are the best of communities brought forth for mankind. (3:110)

Abū Suʿūd describes this verse in his commentary:

> This means the best people *for* others. This is an unambiguous expression which states that the good [mentioned here] lies in benefit provided to the people. This is also understood from the expression, "*brought forth for mankind*"—namely, brought forth to benefit them and advance their best interests.[1]

Our Prophet ﷺ said, "Allah will continue to assist the servant, as long as the servant is assisting his brother."[2] We can thereby understand that divine aid and succor will accrue to this community as long as we are providing the same to fellow members of the human family.

HISTORICAL BASIS FOR INVOLVEMENT

In today's socio-political environment, concern and benefit can be understood as civic involvement. The word "civic" is derived from the word "city." Hence, civic involvement refers to the meaningful ways in which a private citizen is best involved in the life of his or her city. Despite its appearance in a largely agrarian context, if we consider the nature of the dominant means of economic production at the time of its emergence, Islam is best associated with the city. Our Prophet ﷺ is identified with the city. Allah mentions in the Qur'an,

لَآ أُقْسِمُ بِهَـٰذَا ٱلْبَلَدِ ۝ وَأَنتَ حِلٌّۢ بِهَـٰذَا ٱلْبَلَدِ

I swear by this city, and you are a free man of this city. (90:1–2)

The Prophet's migration was from Mecca to Medina, from one city to another. Islamic learning and culture is associated with great cities—Damascus, Baghdad, Cairo, Isfahan, Samarqand, Bukhara, Tashkent, Qayrawan, Fez, Cordova, Seville, Granada, Istanbul, Sarajevo, Zabid, Timbuktu, Delhi, and many others.

It was the involvement of Muslims in the lives of these cities, many of which were established before the arrival of Islam, which defined them in their historical contexts. As Muslims, our involvement in the life of our cities should similarly leave a lasting and positive mark on them. Surely we have much to offer in that regard. This is especially true if we can be people whose lives are changed by the principles and exercises outlined earlier in this *Agenda.* It is not without purpose that Allah has placed us in significant numbers in and around the great metropolises of America. Now is the time for our constructive involvement in the lives of these cities to commence.

Such involvement is especially critical in these times of political transformation and the redefinition of both the role and scope of government here in America. As the two major political parties become increasingly responsive to special interest groups, particularly those associated with big business, large unions, and wealthy individuals, their role as facilitators of democratic and civic involvement is being eroded. This shift in responsiveness is leading to what is referred to as a dealignment of those parties. This dealignment causes private citizens to search for new institutions to serve as their primary means of political involvement, which consequently results in the proliferation of smaller, grassroots civic organizations. The collective weight of these organizations and their facilitation of direct citizen involvement in local politics is viewed by some as the reinventing of American democracy.[3]

POSITION OF MUSLIMS AND CONTRIBUTIONS

The potential contributions of Muslims and the benevolent influence of Islam in this process are tremendous for a number of reasons. In terms of addressing issues associated with poverty, the social welfare policy of both governmental and non-profit organizations has centered on what has been referred to as "a deficit model that focuses on the deficiencies of individuals and communities, rather than building upon the individual, associational, and institutional assets and networks that already exist."[4] This deficit model systematically weakens citizens and communities, as the power of governmental and private agencies ascends. As government retreats from the obligations assumed by the welfare state, the aforementioned organizations are threatened. Hence, the existence of this ineffective model is also threatened. As a result, an opening exists for Muslims to provide an alternative model of civic involvement and activism.

The unique position of Muslims is rooted in the dichotomous nature of our community wherein less affluent, largely minority converts and recent immigrants live in inner cities, while more affluent and established immigrants reside in suburbs. This dichotomy creates a situation in which the Muslims of inner cities have a tremendous potential of *social capital*, or the ability to draw on developed internal communal support systems and networks with other organizations, such as churches, schools, neighborhood associations, local politicians, and small interest groups. On the other hand, Muslims living in the suburbs have tremendous *intellectual and financial capital*. If we could constructively bring these two reservoirs of capital together, we could develop a demonstrable model that could initiate a revolution in American civic participation. That revolution lies in our potential to reverse one of the most damaging implications of suburban sprawl—the depletion of intellectual and material resources from the inner city.

Rudimentary efforts undertaken by Muslims to counter this trend have already begun. Organizations such as the Inner-City Muslim Action Network (IMAN) in Chicago combine the material and intellectual resources of suburban Muslims with the organizational expertise and networking potential of inner-city Muslims to create a dynamic synthesis that is having an ever greater impact on the life of both Muslim and non-Muslim communities. In Los Angeles, the Umma Community Clinic demonstrates how the vision and focused action of suburban university students can create a major center that provides one of the few venues where poor residents of the South Central Los Angeles community can receive free basic medical care and referrals for more advanced treatment. In the Washington, DC area, the Zakat Project initiated by the All Dulles Area Muslim Society (ADAMS) builds bridges of goodwill and helps to initiate avenues of communication and coordination between the wealthy Muslims of suburban northern Virginia and the poorer communities of inner-city Washington, DC. In Richardson, Texas, the Islamic Association of North Texas (IANT) provided the funding to renovate one of the oldest mosques of inner-city Dallas. In Santa Clara, a suburb in the southern San Francisco Bay Area, the Rahima Foundation works in collaboration with Masjid Warithuddin of inner-city Oakland to help feed three hundred families a month.

If we can expand and develop these efforts, a new and unprecedented model of civic involvement can emerge. This development is in no way limited to the social service sector. Mobilized social capital would inevitably engender deeper models of citizen involvement that involve greater forms of self-governance and enhanced collaboration with other economic, social, and political actors.

However, for these developments to occur, we need a revitalized type of Muslim—one who is instilled with a bold and God-conscious vision. This is why the *Agenda to Change Our Condition* is so important. If implemented, it will engender Muslims with a healthier relationship with Allah, and a healthier relationship with Allah will lead to a healthier relationship with our neighbors. That enhanced relationship will in turn lead to a change in our collective condition, God willing.

May blessings and peace be upon the
Messenger of Allah, as long
as those who remember
him continue to
do so . . .

ENDNOTES

1. Abū Suʿūd Muḥammad b. Muḥammad, *Irshād al-ʿuqūl al-salām ilā mazāyā al-Kitāb al-Karīm* (Beirut: Dār al-Kutub al-ʿIlmiyyah, 1999), 2:17.
2. al-Nawawī, *al-Minhāj*, 9:24, no.2793.
3. See Carmen Sirianni and Lewis Friedland, *Civic Innovation in America: Community Empowerment, Public Policy, and the Movement for Civic Renewal* (Berkeley: University of California Press, 2001), p.1.
4. Ibid., p. 11.

APPENDIX A

Foundations of the Spiritual Path: Sīdī Aḥmad Zarrūq

The noble scholar, unrivaled in his time, leader of scholars and saints, Sīdī Aḥmad Zarrūq al-Barnūsī al-Fāsī ﷺ (d.1493) *says:*

If anyone is asked about the foundations of his path, he should reply:

The foundations of our path are five:

- mindfulness of Allah privately and publicly;
- adherence to the Sunnah[1] in word and deed;
- indifference to the acceptance or rejection of others;
- satisfaction with Allah in hardship and ease; and
- turning to Allah in prosperity and adversity.

Mindfulness of Allah is realized through scrupulousness and uprightness; adherence to the Sunnah, through caution and excellent character; indifference to the acceptance or rejection of others, through patience and trust; satisfaction, through acceptance of what one is given and consignment of one's affairs to Allah; turning to Allah, through praise and gratitude in times of prosperity and through asylum with Allah in times of affliction.

The foundations of the preceding five are predicated on the following five:

- possessing celestial aspirations;
- preserving reverence for Allah;
- excelling in service of others;
- fulfilling one's resolves; and
- exalting one's blessings.

When one aspires to heights, one's station rises. When one preserves Allah's sanctity, one's sanctity is preserved. When one excels in service, one's standing is assured. When one fulfills resolutions, one's guidance continues. When one exalts blessings, one is grateful, and gratitude ensures increase from the Ever-Giving in accord with His sincere promise.

The foundations of proper conduct are five:

- pursuing knowledge to fulfill this sacred affair;
- accompanying a spiritual guide and a fraternity to gain insight;
- abandoning dispensations and excuses for one's own protection;
- managing one's time for litanies that result in presence of heart; and
- guarding against the ego to free it of whims and save it from destructive tendencies.

The pitfall of academic pursuit is the company of the immature, either in age, understanding, or devotional practice, from among the unprincipled and ungrounded; the pitfall of spiritual company is arrogance, deception, and meddling in the affairs of others;[2] the pitfall of forgoing dispensations and excuses is self-pity; the pitfall of managing time for litanies is spectacle and ritualized devotion;[3] the pitfall of guarding against the ego is complacency due to its excellence and probity. Indeed, Allah says, *Even if he paid every ransom, none would be accepted from him* (6:70); and the noble son of the noble, Joseph ﷺ, the son of Jacob ﷺ said, "*I do not exonerate myself; for the self is certainly compulsive with evil unless my Lord has mercy*" (12:53).

The foundations of treatment for the illnesses of the soul are five:

- relieving digestion by reducing the amount of food;
- seeking asylum with Allah from harm at the time of its occurrence;
- shunning places where one fears misdeeds will occur;
- continual repentance coupled with prayers upon the

Prophet ﷺ in solitude and society; and
- accompanying a guide to Allah or to the affair of Allah; unfortunately, such a person no longer exists.[4]

Abū al-Ḥasan al-Shādhilī (d.1258) said,

> My beloved counseled me not to set foot in a place unless I expected a divine recompense; nor to sit in a place unless I felt safe from sin; nor to accompany anyone unless I found him supporting my duties to Allah; and not to select anyone as a friend unless he increased my certainty. And how rare such people are!

He also said, "Whoever directs you to the ephemeral cheats you; whoever directs you to activity exhausts you; but whoever directs you to Allah counsels you." Furthermore, he said, "Make mindfulness of Allah your abode, and the delight of your ego will do you no harm, as long as it is not content with vice, nor persists in sin, and you do not lose your awareness of Allah in private."

I say complacency, persistent sin, and negligence of Allah in solitude are the roots of all calamities, pitfalls, and faults. They, in turn, engender five afflictions:

- preferring ignorance over knowledge;
- being duped by every spiritual charlatan;
- neglecting one's duty in important matters;
- exulting in the spiritual path; and
- hastening spiritual openings without fulfilling their conditions.

These foster five other afflictions:

- preferring innovations to the Sunnah;
- imitating vacuous people instead of those of substance;
- behaving capriciously in both trivial and weighty matters;
- preferring fantasies over realities; and
- declaring insincere claims.

From these last five, another five manifest:

- having obsessive-compulsive thoughts during worship;
- overindulging in normal human activities;

- gathering ritually for invocation and chanting;
- drawing attention to oneself at every opportunity; and
- accompanying worldlings, even mixing with members of the opposite sex and adolescents,[5] deluded by events that happened to genuine Sufis, and then making mention of their judgments as justification.

Obsessive-compulsive thoughts arise from innovation, the basis of which is ignorance of the Sunnah or some psychological affliction.

[As for those overindulging in worldly matters], had they realized, they would know that worldly engagements are a dispensation due to human frailties, and should be limited to the necessities of life, nothing more. Indeed, they are actually remedies and are a way of fulfilling the right of divine wisdom in such affairs. No one is unrestrained in worldly pursuits unless he or she is far from Allah.

As for devotional gatherings, they are permitted for people overpowered by their states or as a respite for people of excellent character. Indeed, such practice is akin to alighting upon the carpet of truth if done according to its conditions, among suitable people, and in an appropriate place—not to mention fulfilling its required courtesies and protocols.

Resorting to creation is eschewing reality, especially when one resorts to an obsequious pedant, a thoughtless tyrant, or an ignorant Sufi. The company of the immature is oppressive and both a worldly and otherworldly fault. But the acceptance of such company is far, far worse. Shaykh Abū Madyan (d.1198) said, "'Immature' means anyone not conforming to the spiritual path you are on, even if he is ninety years of age." I say, an immature person is one who never persists in anything but jumps at each new occurrence and is impassioned by it. You generally find such a person among the devotees of the path,[6] meaning the various spiritual groups and seekers of congregations. So avoid them to the utmost of your ability.

Anyone who claims to have a station with Allah yet reveals any of the following five is either a liar or is deluded:

- using one's limbs in sinful acts;
- feigning piety;
- desiring the ephemeral world;
- speaking ill of Allah's servants; or
- lacking the respect that Allah commands toward all Muslims.

Such people rarely die in a state of grace.

The qualifications of the spiritual guide with whom the seeker may safely entrust his soul are five:

- unadulterated spiritual experience;
- sound outward knowledge;
- celestial aspirations;
- a pleasing state; and
- penetrating spiritual discernment.

Whoever has any of these five cannot be a true spiritual guide:

- ignorance of the religion;
- disregard for the reverence of other Muslims;
- meddling in matters that do not concern him;
- following whims in everything; or
- remorseless displays of lack of comportment.

The courtesies of a student with his or her spiritual guide and fellow wayfarers are also five:

- following the directions of the guide, even if contrary to one's own preference;
- avoiding what one's guide forbids, even if doing so seems highly adverse;
- honoring one's guide when he is present or absent, alive or dead;
- fulfilling his rights, to the best of one's ability, without neglect; and
- abandoning one's understanding, knowledge, and leadership to that of the guide, unless these are already in accord with one's guide.[7]

Should the seeker find a guide who lacks any of the five aforementioned qualifications of a true spiritual teacher, he should depend on the incomplete guide only in those areas in which he is qualified. The seeker should treat him like a brother in regard to the neglected areas.

Thus ends the *Five Foundations* with the praise, help, and perfect success of Allah.

It is necessary to read this text every day, once or twice. If that is not possible, then at least once a week until its meanings are imprinted on one's soul and are manifest in one's behavior. Indeed, it contains enough to dispense with many books and much advice. And, as the saying goes, "Whoever neglects the foundations, is prevented from reaching the goal." The one who reflects deeply on what we have said will acknowledge its truth, continue to have recourse to it, and use it as a reminder. Success is ultimately by Allah.

ENDNOTES

1. In his book of definitions, Imam al-Jurjānī (d. 1413) says regarding the Sunnah, "In sacred law, it refers to a normative practice of the religion aside from that which is obligatory. Thus, the Sunnah is what the Prophet ﷺ practiced habitually, even if he sometimes omitted it. If the Prophet ﷺ performed the practice devotionally, then it is considered a revealed Sunnah (*sunan al-hudā*). If the practice was his personal wont, then it is considered a supplemental Sunnah (*sunan al-zawā'id*). The revealed *sunan* are those that complete one's religious practice, and neglecting them is discouraged and inappropriate. As for the supplemental *sunan*, their practice is considered virtuous but not necessary. If one chooses not to practice them, there is no blame or dereliction; these involve such actions as the way the Prophet ﷺ walked, sat, dressed, and ate.

2. The word glossed as "meddling" is *fuḍūl*, which means "the quality of busying oneself with that which does not concern one." Often, those living in spiritual communities are engaged in the constant service of others; in such an environment, one can easily become the spiritual busybody who is preoccupied with everyone's salvation but his own.

3. One manuscript reads, "The pitfall of managing time for litanies is preoccupation with recommended actions [to the detriment of more urgent priorities]."

4. Sīdī Aḥmad Zarrūq, while a master of this science, believed that authentic teachers of the art of self-mastery and divine knowledge were no longer present by the fifteenth century CE. Ibn ʿAjībah (d. 1809) differed with him on this point and believed the earth is never devoid of those who guide to God until the end of time, as this is the real purpose of the human project. Their difference, however, is more semantic than substantial; Sīdī Aḥmad Zarrūq does not mean that teachers no longer exist, but is referring to teachers of the caliber and stature of al-Junayd (d.910) and al-Shādhilī (d.1258), and also mentions this point as a warning to people seeking teachers, as spiritual imposters abound in every age.

5. "Adolescents" here refers to youth other than one's own children.

6. The author refers here to Sufi fraternities (*ṭuruq*). While he was, in fact, a member of the Shādhilī path, he recognized an inherent group mentality that afflicts many of those engaged in such activities; here, he warns against people who have this tendency. Many people join such groups not for real spiritual work but simply to be part of a "group" or

to dabble in spiritual matters, a common human propensity; but such people can waste the time of and be obstacles for serious practitioners. For an interesting study of this type of personality, see the section on "dabblers" from George Leonard's, *Mastery: The Keys to Success and Long-Term Fulfillment* (New York: Penguin Books, 1992).

7. This does not mean surrendering one's sovereignty to another person, as the relationship of a subject to a tyrant; rather, the student forgoes the ego's desire to constantly lead and be in control. A true guide does not cultivate a controlling relationship based upon despotic models of domination. On the other hand, even in the world of material travel, a guide cannot lead someone who has hired him if he refuses to follow his directions. The best model is the Prophet's relationship with his companions; hence a guide should exemplify the prophetic character. Al-Ḥabīb Aḥmad Mashhūr al-Ḥaddād (d.1995), who was a living exemplar of this tradition, treated his disciples with utmost love, respect, and deference, and they in turn reciprocated.

APPENDIX B

The Counsel of Imam al-Nawawī

SECTION CONCERNING ARRIVAL TO THE KNOWLEDGE OF ALLAH

There is a large portion about the path to Allah that appears in the great Imam al-Nawawī's al Maqāṣid; *it is a wonderfully succinct summation of the path to Allah. Imam al-Nawawī* ﷺ *(*d.1277*) writes the following:*

[Arrival to the knowledge of Allah is achieved] by repenting from all things unlawful or offensive; seeking sacred knowledge in accordance with one's needs; maintaining ritual purity; performing the obligatory prayers in the first of their time and in congregation, as well as the Sunnah prayers that correspond to each of the obligatory prayers; adhering to the eight units (*rakaʿāt*) of the midmorning (*ḍuḥā*) prayer and the six units after the sunset (*maghrib*) prayer and before the night (*ʿishā'*) prayer; performing the late night (*tahajjud*) prayers after awaking from one's sleep; fulfilling the *witr* prayer; fasting on Mondays and Thursdays, and on the three days of the full moon—i.e., the 13th, 14th, and 15th of the lunar month—and also on the other days of the year in which fasting is recommended; reciting the Qur'an with the heart's presence, coupled with reflection upon its meanings; frequently asking forgiveness of Allah; maintaining prayers and blessings upon the Prophet ﷺ; and, finally, adhering to the meritorious invocations of the morning and the evening that have been transmitted to us from the Sunnah.

APPENDIX C

The Counsel of Sīdī Aḥmad Zarrūq

EXCERPTS FROM THE *POOR MAN'S BOOK OF ASSISTANCE* (*Kitāb al-iʿānah*)

Sīdī Aḥmad Zarrūq ﷺ *writes*:

May Allah give you and us success, rectify our worldly and otherworldly lives, and grant us adherence to the way of the truth in our journeys and our sojourns. Know that repentance is a key, mindfulness of Allah is vast, and uprightness is the source of rectification. Meanwhile, a servant is never free of blunders, shortcomings, or lassitude. Therefore, never be neglectful of repentance; never be remiss in your return to Allah; and never neglect acts that bring you closer to Allah. Indeed, any time you are remiss in fulfilling any of these three duties, still repent and return; anytime you err, hear and obey; anytime you fall short or burn out, do not give up. Let your concern be emptying yourself of vices, and then continue to work on your outward state through counseling.

Be steadfast in this practice until you find that fleeing from vices is second nature and that your respect for sacred limits is as if a protective net surrounds you. At this point, it is time to turn inward toward your heart's presence and to its reality with both reflection and remembrance. Do not hasten the end without mastery of the outset; likewise, do not stop at the outset without the end in sight; for anyone who needs at the end what one must acquire at the outset loses grace, while anyone who attempts to achieve the end at the outset loses guidance.

Act with principles and legalities, not with stories and assumptions. Do not bother with stories, except as a tonic to strengthen your resolve, but certainly not as a reference or as a basis of benefit. Rather, adhere to a clear path to which you can always refer and a foundation upon which you can, in your various conditions, always rely. Among the paths, the most virtuous is that of Ibn ʿAṭā' Allāh (d.1309) due to its clear direction to Allah.[1] Do not use the doctrine of other paths, unless they accord with your own; but accept what they imply if you desire realization. Abandon foul speech completely. Cast off anything if you fail to sense its benefit immediately. Beware of being too hard on your self (*nafs*) before you have mastered it. Contrariwise, beware of being too lax with it concerning its obligations. Indeed, the self by its nature is forever fleeing from moderation. In fact, it desires the extreme in both vice and virtue.

Find a sincere friend whom you can rely upon in your spiritual pursuit, one with whom you can discuss whatever is happening to you inwardly and outwardly. Should you accompany such a person, treat him based upon his state, only giving of yourself in accord with his shortcomings and perfected qualities, because a complete sincere friend no longer exists. Indeed, in these times, even a suitable companion who is agreeable rarely lasts. Furthermore, beware of the majority of people concerning both your religious and worldly affairs, unless you have ascertained that they have a sound relationship with their Lord, which is rooted in knowledge, unaccompanied by caprice or power issues. They should also have a sound intellect that is free of the pitfalls of hidden agendas. Do not be heedless of the machinations of others or their hidden states. Consider these two qualities from both their origins and their actions. People of high character and family distinction are almost always beneficial; on the other hand, excruciating circumstances compel a person of low character and origin to forsake others in need.

Be aware of the dominant qualities of a given people in a given land, as you should not neglect the divine wisdom in creation. Discern the unity in the essence of diversity. Some of this we have already covered in the book, *The Principles* (*al-Qawāʿid*), so study the subject further there.

Manage your time suitably, using a gentle and tolerant approach. Beware of both harshness and self-indulgence. Self-indulgence in the merely permissible sets the heart back on its journey to such a degree that even a man of resolve may end up looking like a foolish child.

"Work for this world as if you will live forever, but work for the next life as if you will die tomorrow." This means you should neither neglect the externalities of this world nor should you be heedless of your end and final destination. Avoid positions of authority to your utmost. If one should befall you, however, know your limitations and, for the sake of Allah, be as guileless as he who knows the One who is, in reality, placing demands on him. Surrender completely to His decree with the submission of one who knows he can never overcome Him. Have a firm foundation in all of your affairs, and you will be safe from their pitfalls. Organize your devotional practices, and you will find your time is extended due to the grace that pervades it.

Never be fanatical about anything, whether true or false, and your heart will maintain its integrity toward others. Never claim anything to which you are entitled, not to mention that to which you are not entitled, and you will be safe from connivance and treachery. Indeed, anyone claiming a rank above his own will fall, scandalized and humiliated. Even still, those who claim a rank they warrant will have it stripped from them. Conversely, those who claim a lesser rank than their own will be elevated to an even higher one than they deserve.

Never reveal to your companion anything of your state other than what his own state warrants. If, on one hand, you condescend to his state, he will disregard you; while on the other hand, if you attempt to elevate him to your state, he will abandon you.

Never demand a right from anyone, whether a relative or a stranger, for the simple reason that a stranger owes you nothing, and a relative is far too important to direct your blame at. Never assume that anyone in this world can really understand your circumstances other than from their own perspective. People perceive things based only upon their personal frames of reference and their personal experiences. However, when aims, purposes, and aspirations are similar, people tend to work together toward a common goal.

Never belittle any discussion about people in their absence, even what appears to be harmless, due to the harm that can result from it. Guard your secrets, even if you feel safe with someone, because the one to whom you divulge your secret is not a safer vessel than your own heart before you revealed it.

Never leave an atom's weight of your regular devotional practice. Never be lenient with yourself in either lax times or resolute ones. Indeed, whenever you miss a time-specific practice, complete it at another time. If you are not able to do your usual practice, at least occupy yourself with some other similar practice. Never obey your selfish soul, even for a moment, nor believe any of its claims, no matter what it says. In all your affairs, guard your resolutions. Should you resolve to do something virtuous, do it without delay before the resolve abates. Scrutinize your ego concerning matters of duty and requests. Do not do anything you do not need to do, even if it is virtuous. In short, do not involve yourself in anything other than the absolutely necessary or that in which a real discernible need exists.

Treat others just as you would want to be treated, and fulfill what is due. All of this is epitomized in the words of the poet when he said,

If you desire to live such that your religion is safe
And your portion is full and your honor is sound,

Guard your tongue; never mention another's faults,
For you too have faults and others have tongues.

Beware your eye should it reveal another's faults,
And say, "O eye, remember the eyes of others!"

Live treating well all others and avoid aggression;
And should they oppress, repel it but with kindness.

These words are taken from the saying of the Prophet ﷺ: "Be aware of Allah wherever you are. Follow up a wrong with a right, and it will repel it. Finally, treat people with utter respect and courtesy." And from his saying, "Every child of Adam makes mistakes, and the best of those who make mistakes are those who seek to redress them." And finally from the Messenger's words, "The Holy Spirit inspired my heart's core that no soul will die until it completes its kismet and allotted time, so be conscious of Allah and dignified in your requests."

In summation, repentance, awareness of Allah, and uprightness are the foundations of all benefits. The truth is manifest, and its details are weighty and significant. The affair belongs to Allah. Success is in His Hands. Peace.

EXCERPTS FROM SĪDĪ AḤMAD ZARRŪQ'S *THE PRINCIPLES* (*al-Qawāʿid*)

Sīdī Aḥmad Zarrūq quotes his teacher, Shaykh Abū al-ʿAbbās al-Ḥaḍramī (d.1495):

Spiritual training was elevated [to a science] due to the development of a technical vocabulary, but nothing remains except benefit derived from aspiration and spiritual states. Therefore, adhere to the Book and the Sunnah without omission or addition. This applies to all of your transactions with your Creator, the creation, and yourself.

Transactions with Allah involve three obligations: adhering to legalities, avoiding prohibitions, and resigning oneself to divine decrees. Also, dealing with the ego has three necessities: fairness with the truth; forgoing justifications; and wariness of the ego and its machinations when involving its desires and aversions, acceptance and rejection, and attractions and antipathies. And finally, dealing with people also has three conditions: fulfilling their rights; eschewing covetousness of their possessions; and restraining from anything that adversely affects their hearts, unless it involves an obligation to the truth that cannot be ignored.

Ruined and hopeless is the disciple[2] who inclines toward the frivolities of equitation;[3] or prefers self-interests; or engages in redressing social wrongs or fighting in military jihads while neglecting the acquisition of personal merit and virtue; or believes he does not need to rectify his own soul or that he can perfect all the virtues; or finds faults in his brothers and others; or claims exemption from worldly obligations due to his spiritual pursuits; or spends all of his time in devotional gatherings; or constantly engages in social groups and gatherings that do not involve teaching or learning; or inclines toward affluent worldlings, claiming that doing so is for religious reasons; or preoccupies himself with spiritual matters of the heart before learning the basics of sound transactions or rectifying his faults; or thrusts himself upon others as a spiritual teacher without a true spiritual master, scholar, or imam appointing him; or mindlessly follows anyone who says, "follow me," irrespective of the veracity of his claims or details of his state; or belittles anyone associated with the people of Allah, even if he deems them insincere with proofs; or inclines toward dispensations and interpretations; or puts the inward ahead of the outward; or is satisfied with the externals to the detriment of the inward; or takes from one what contradicts the other; or is content with knowledge devoid of action or with action devoid of a spiritual state or knowledge; or is content with a spiritual state and ignores the other two; or regarding his actions, knowledge, states, or practices has no reference from the seminal texts to which he can refer, such as the books of Ibn ʿAṭā' Allāh concerning inward matters—especially *The Illumination* (*al-Tanwīr*)—and, concerning outward manners, Ibn al-Ḥājj's (d.1337) *The Introduction* (*al-Madkhal*), and the books of his shaykh, Ibn Abī Jamrah (d.1299), and others who follow the same path among the realized masters. Any disciple engaged in such things is ruined and hopeless. Whoever holds, however, to the Book and the Sunnah will be safe and will, Godspeed, arrive. Protection is from Him alone, and success is by Him.

The Messenger of Allah ﷺ was once asked about Allah's words, *Tend to your own souls* (5:105).

He replied, "If you see covetousness obeyed, passions and whims followed, and every opinionated person marveling at his own opinions, then tend to your own soul."

He also said something to this effect:

> It is written in the scrolls of Abraham ﷺ that, "An intelligent person should know the age in which he lives; he should hold his tongue and mind his own business. An intelligent person should have four portions to his day, each portion as follows: a portion to take his soul to account, a portion to converse with his Lord, a portion to spend time with his brothers—meaning those who help him to see clearly his faults and direct him to his Lord—and a portion to indulge in his own personal recreation from the permissible appetites of man."

May Allah provide us with that and help us to fulfill it. May He always maintain us in a state of grace, for we cannot survive without His bestowal of grace and prosperity. Allah is enough for us, and Allah is the best of protectors. May blessings and peace be upon our master Muḥammad ﷺ and his family and his companions.

ENDNOTES

1. The author is referring to the Shādhilī path (*ṭarīqah*), which is known as "the scholar's way." It focuses on a strong exoteric doctrine and adherence to the sacred law, coupled with a more experiential esoteric doctrine as opposed to some of the more philosophical paths found in Spain and in the East.

2. A disciple (*murīd*) is someone who has entered into a covenant with a master in hopes of acquiring true prophetic character and obtaining experiential knowledge of God. Sīdī Aḥmad Zarrūq's warnings that follow apply to any serious spiritual aspirant who desires to move quickly on the spiritual path.

3. Equitation, or horsemanship, was a sport of the aristocracy in Sīdī Aḥmad Zarrūq's time. Modern equivalents include racing and collecting automobiles. Many wealthy people today have several luxury cars, including classic models, and spend an inordinate amount of time with them. Such frivolous activities are spiritually lethal.

ALL APPENDICES TRANSLATED
BY HAMZA YUSUF

EXERCISES

GUARDING THE PRAYER

Of all the actions that a Muslim will do in his or her life, none is more important than the five prescribed prayers. It is the central pillar that supports the entire edifice of Islam.

It is the prayer that is the believer's protection and it is his connection with his Lord. The prayer is a science and an art that takes many years of serious and vigilant practice in order to arrive at its true reality.

The exercise may take several years to complete, but this is the struggle of the believer, so do not despair. For a man, this exercise is preferably done in congregation, but due to the fact that many people do not live near a mosque in Western countries, this is not always an option.

Make a Vow With Allah

Each morning, vow to Allah that you will pray the five prescribed prayers on time and fulfill their conditions, pillars, near integrals, and recommended acts.

Guard Your Vow

Be vigilant about all your prayers, particularly the dawn prayer, the middle prayer, and the sunset prayer, as they are the most easily missed.

Take Yourself to Account

At the end of the day, if you keep your vow, place a mark in the chart below. If, on the other hand, you did not fulfill your vow, then go back to day one and start over. Ask for forgiveness and strength in fulfilling it for the next day, and give some charity, fast, or do some other type of punitive measure to discipline your soul.

1	2	3	4	5	6	7	8
9	10	11	12	13	14	15	16
17	18	19	20	21	22	23	24
25	26	27	28	29	30	31	32
33	34	35	36	37	38	39	40

GUARDING THE TONGUE

The tongue has only one noble quality and that is truthfulness. On the other hand, it has over twenty destructive qualities, but their sources are rooted in the following four: Lying, Backbiting, Argumentation, and Engaging in what does not concern you.

Be firm with others that you do not want to listen to these things either. If it means losing a friend who is not willing to change with you for the better, then so be it.

Finally, remember that writing falls into these categories and that the internet is infested with lies, slander, argumentation and engagement in matters of no concern. Therefore, you should include writing in your vow also.

Make a Vow With Allah

Each morning, make a commitment not to lie, backbite, argue, or speak of matters that do not concern you. Be firm with others that you do not want to listen to these things either.

Guard Your Vow

Throughout the day, be vigilant in your observation and note the times when you do not fulfill the condition. This is guarding the condition.

Take Yourself to Account

At the end of the day, if you keep your vow, place a mark in the chart below. If, on the other hand, you did not fulfill your vow, then go back to day one and start over. Ask for forgiveness and strength in fulfilling it for the next day, and give some charity, fast, or do some other type of punitive measure to discipline your soul.

1	2	3	4	5	6	7	8
9	10	11	12	13	14	15	16
17	18	19	20	21	22	23	24
25	26	27	28	29	30	31	32
33	34	35	36	37	38	39	40

GUARDING THE PRAYER

Of all the actions that a Muslim will do in his or her life, none is more important than the five prescribed prayers. It is the central pillar that supports the entire edifice of Islam.

It is the prayer that is the believer's protection and it is his connection with his Lord. The prayer is a science and an art that takes many years of serious and vigilant practice in order to arrive at its true reality.

The exercise may take several years to complete, but this is the struggle of the believer, so do not despair. For a man, this exercise is preferably done in congregation, but due to the fact that many people do not live near a mosque in Western countries, this is not always an option.

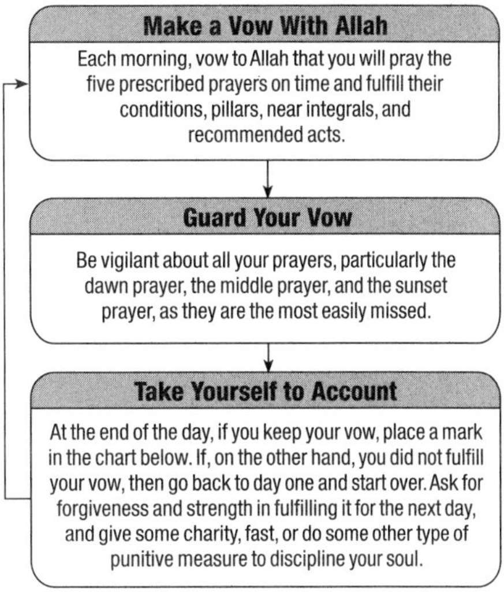

1	2	3	4	5	6	7	8
9	10	11	12	13	14	15	16
17	18	19	20	21	22	23	24
25	26	27	28	29	30	31	32
33	34	35	36	37	38	39	40

GUARDING THE TONGUE

The tongue has only one noble quality and that is truthfulness. On the other hand, it has over twenty destructive qualities, but their sources are rooted in the following four: Backbiting, Argumentation, and Engaging in what does not concern you.

Be firm with others that you do not want to listen to these things either. If it means losing a friend who is not willing to change with you for the better, then so be it.

Finally, remember that writing falls into these categories and that the internet is infested with lies, slander, argumentation and engagement in matters of no concern. Therefore, you should include writing in your vow also.

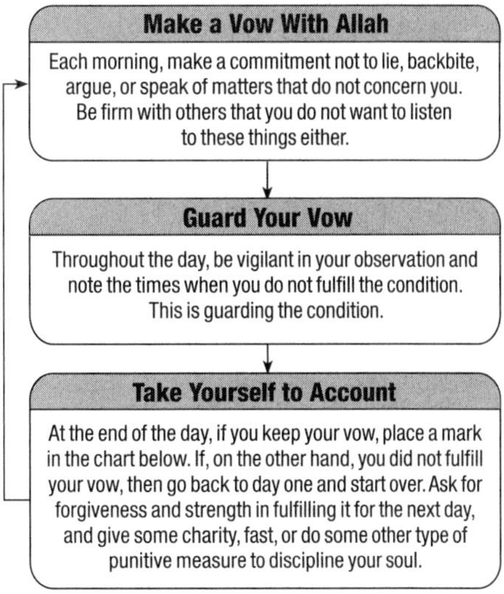

1	2	3	4	5	6	7	8
9	10	11	12	13	14	15	16
17	18	19	20	21	22	23	24
25	26	27	28	29	30	31	32
33	34	35	36	37	38	39	40

GUARDING THE STOMACH

Guarding the stomach is perhaps the most important of the exercises. Some may even want to begin with this exercise, particularly those who are eating foods that are clearly prohibited, such as those produced or purchased with unlawful income.

The commentators say that there is a direct relation between doing righteous works and eating pure foods. In this context, purity means that both the food itself and its source are pure.

During this exercise, one should focus on removing any prohibited food substances or sources. Learning to control the appetite is one of the most powerful means to controlling the self and achieving God-consciousness.

Make a Vow With Allah

Each morning, vow to Allah that you will eat what is permissible and pure, and avoid excess eating as well as unwholesome foods.

Guard Your Vow

Don't overeat. make sure that you eat food that is permissible. Our Prophet ﷺ said, "Leave what gives you doubt for what does not give you doubt."

Take Yourself to Account

At the end of the day, if you keep your vow, place a mark in the chart below. If, on the other hand, you did not fulfill your vow, then go back to day one and start over. Ask for forgiveness and strength in fulfilling it for the next day, and give some charity, fast, or do some other type of punitive measure to discipline your soul.

1	2	3	4	5	6	7	8
9	10	11	12	13	14	15	16
17	18	19	20	21	22	23	24
25	26	27	28	29	30	31	32
33	34	35	36	37	38	39	40

GUARDING THE PRIVATE PARTS

Guarding the private parts simply entails avoiding places of temptation and possible harm. One should never, under any circumstances, be alone with someone of the opposite sex unless there are legal relations present, such as one's spouse or direct relatives.

For the believer, this should be the easiest of the exercises, if he or she follows the simple rule of never being alone with someone of the opposite sex who is unrelated to him or her. The Prophet ﷺ said, "Whoever guards for me his tongue and private parts, I can guarantee him a place in the Garden."

One should also guard one's nakedness and avoid any displays of what is prohibited for others to see.

Make a Vow With Allah

Each morning, vow to Allah that you will guard your private parts and avoid being alone with members of the opposite sex who are unrelated to you.

Guard Your Vow

Be aware of your conduct throughout the day. Maintain vigilance, as sexual appetite is one of Satan's greatest weapons.

Take Yourself to Account

At the end of the day, if you keep your vow, place a mark in the chart below. If, on the other hand, you did not fulfill your vow, then go back to day one and start over. Ask for forgiveness and strength in fulfilling it for the next day, and give some charity, fast, or do some other type of punitive measure to discipline your soul.

1	2	3	4	5	6	7	8
9	10	11	12	13	14	15	16
17	18	19	20	21	22	23	24
25	26	27	28	29	30	31	32
33	34	35	36	37	38	39	40

GUARDING THE HANDS

The blessed Messenger of Allah ﷺ said, "The Muslim is one from whose tongue and hands other Muslims are safe." This means protecting the hands from stealing from or harming any part of Allah's creation without just right.

We should never raise our hands to any Muslim unless it is in self-defense, nor should we do so to any non-Muslim unless it is in self-defense, in a legitimate struggle for the defense of homeland, or a jihad under the legitimate authority of the leader of the Muslims. Even in war, Muslims should never kill a woman, child, old person, or non-combatants. We should not use our hands to sow any corruption in the earth.

Make a Vow With Allah

Each morning, vow to Allah that you will not use your hands to commit wrong actions, sow corruption in the earth, steal, or cause harm to any part of God's creation without just right.

Guard Your Vow

Throughout the day, be vigilant in the controlling of your hands, and note the times and conditions when you do not fulfill your vow.

Take Yourself to Account

At the end of the day, if you keep your vow, place a mark in the chart below. If, on the other hand, you did not fulfill your vow, then go back to day one and start over. Ask for forgiveness and strength in fulfilling it for the next day, and give some charity, fast, or do some other type of punitive measure to discipline your soul.

1	2	3	4	5	6	7	8
9	10	11	12	13	14	15	16
17	18	19	20	21	22	23	24
25	26	27	28	29	30	31	32
33	34	35	36	37	38	39	40

GUARDING THE FEET

Our feet are our means of mobility, and therefore we should consider driving or traveling by any means as actions of the feet. We should apply this standard to all endeavors that we undertake. For the most part, things are permissible. Allah has made very few things prohibitied. We are obliged to learn what is prohibited and then avoid them.

When we set out to a place, we should recite the prayer of the blessed Prophet Muhammad ﷺ:

"O Allah, I seek refuge in You that I should go astray or lead others astray, that I should trip or trip up others, that I should oppress or be oppressed, or that I should grow ignorance or be the brunt of ignorance."

Make a Vow With Allah

Each morning, vow to Allah that you will reflect on your travels and avoid places and situations that are prohibited.

Guard Your Vow

Avoid going to places where people are committing prohibitions and where you are likely to commit wrong actions.

Take Yourself to Account

At the end of the day, if you keep your vow, place a mark in the chart below. If, on the other hand, you did not fulfill your vow, then go back to day one and start over. Ask for forgiveness and strength in fulfilling it for the next day, and give some charity, fast, or do some other type of punitive measure to discipline your soul.

1	2	3	4	5	6	7	8
9	10	11	12	13	14	15	16
17	18	19	20	21	22	23	24
25	26	27	28	29	30	31	32
33	34	35	36	37	38	39	40